The Eiffel Tower

An early promotional illustration of the Eiffel Tower before its construction.

The Eiffel Tower

Symbol of an Age

JOSEPH HARRISS

Paul Elek   London

Published in Great Britain 1976 by
Elek Books Ltd
54-58 Caledonian Road, London N1 9RN

First published in the United States of America 1975
by Houghton Mifflin Company as *The Tallest Tower*.

ISBN 0 236 40036 3

Printed in Great Britain by Unwin Brothers Limited
The Gresham Press, Old Woking, Surrey, England.
A member of the Staples Printing Group

To the memory of my father

CONTENTS

ILLUSTRATIONS

The Eiffel Tower

PROLOGUE

FRANCE'S THIRD REPUBLIC was conceived in the confused aftermath of the country's humiliating defeat by the Prussians in 1870. It perished sixty-nine years and 107 governments later, in the debacle of yet another abject capitulation. Between those worst of times, however, French citizens lived in what we now think of nostalgically as one of the best of times.

The Belle Epoque, like the Renaissance and other labels bestowed by historians, was not a pat, monolithic era. It was a tumultuous time of tension and contradiction, change and anticipation, much like our own. But it does appear that there was a period toward the end of the last century when new prosperity and old values fused briefly to produce an era in many ways happier, or at least more sure of itself, than any we have known since. This was the age that, with a remarkable sense of itself, created the Eiffel Tower. A synthesis of technics and mood, this bizarre structure became the epitome of its time: a compendium of engineering methods and materials developed during the first century of the Industrial Revolution, it is also the most expressive statement of how one part of the human race felt about itself at one point in its history.

1

ONE

THE FRENCH were not alone in enjoying the momentary state of grace known as the Belle Epoque. Most of northwestern Europe and the northeastern United States experienced it in recognizably similar form. But if France's euphoria in the last years of the nineteenth century appears heightened, the impression is perhaps due to a backdrop of travail. For the Franco-Prussian War, in which the Imperial Army of Napoleon III was smashed in a matter of weeks, was not merely a military defeat. The war led to the loss of France's eastern provinces of Alsace and Lorraine, with a population of nearly a million and a half, economically vital mines and industries and the great city of Strasbourg. Moreover, the settlement President Adolphe Thiers made with the Germans in February 1871 involved an enormous and debilitating indemnity of five billion francs, or about one billion dollars, and stipulated that German troops would occupy the country's eastern departments until the sum had been paid.

Parisians in particular had borne much of the brunt of the war, undergoing a five-month siege during which they were reduced to eating cats, rats and the animals in their zoos. No sooner had peace been concluded than the revolt of the Paris Commune broke out on March 18. A political insurrection in the image of those that had shaken Paris sporadically for a century, the Commune revolt was sparked when Thiers suspended payment to national guardsmen — the only income of many families because of the severe unemployment at the time — and ended a moratorium on rents and bills. Moreover, Parisians felt increasingly isolated and misunderstood when the National Assembly moved to Versailles to escape the seething resentment of the capital. The national guardsmen of Montmartre and Belleville refused to yield their weapons, including over 200 cannons, when ordered to disarm. The independent, self-governing Commune of Paris was proclaimed, and for two months the city was ravaged by fire and divided by barricades as 30,000 Communards held out against 130,000 government troops. When Marshal MacMahon's army finally quelled the revolt after bloody street fighting, nearly 20,000 Parisians had died at the hands of their compatriots and entire areas of the city lay in ruins.

As the stunned city began to put itself back together, it first had to overcome its own divisive tendencies. Of the National Assembly elected in 1871, nearly 400 of 650 members were monarchists dedicated to ending the Republic as soon as they could decide who would be king. Unable to choose among the Comte de Chambord, the Comte de Paris and a possible Bonaparte, however, the Assembly reluctantly gave birth to the Republic because, as President Thiers said later, "It divided us least." A period of political confusion had begun — there would be twelve governments over the next eight years alone — but the Republic survived. Ironically, the nation's conservative elements, the peasantry and the haute bourgeoisie, would preserve it.

France went to work on its problems, first of all paying off the indemnity much more rapidly than anyone had foreseen thanks to the enthusiastic response of French investors to the government's bond issues. Two billion francs were paid in July 1871, permitting evacuation of German troops from five of twenty-one occupied departments. By March 1873, another half-billion francs were paid, and the rest of the debt was liquidated in monthly installments. The remaining German soldiers left in September, a year ahead of schedule, and by 1875 France had already balanced its budget. The nation began healing its self-inflicted wounds as well. It ceased looking back toward the ancien régime when MacMahon resigned as president in January 1879, to be replaced by a thoroughly bourgeois republican lawyer, Jules Grévy. A full amnesty for the thousands of Communard prisoners or exiles was granted in 1880, a year after the government had felt secure enough to make "The Marseillaise" the national anthem and to move the Chamber of Deputies and the Senate back to Paris from Versailles.

As the economy gained momentum, the standard of living improved rapidly. National income nearly doubled in the four decades following 1870; industrial production tripled and foreign trade increased 75 percent. To the chagrin of German geologists who in 1871 had laid out the boundaries of Lorraine in such a way as to annex all known iron deposits, France discovered it had the largest iron vein in Europe on its side of the border, reserves estimated at almost one-fifth of the world's supply. During the 1880s France gradually conquered a colonial empire in Indochina and North and Central Africa that was to become second only to Great Britain's in terms of population and size and would be an enormous new market for French investment and industrial output.

It was altogether an amazing comeback from military defeat and incipient civil war which France had effected in the space of little more than a decade. With the Republic firmly established and the nation once again a prosperous world power, the government began looking forward to commemorating the centennial of the French Revolution. As early as 1878, several cabinet ministers were gestating the idea of a purely national industrial exhibition to be held in 1889.

In truth, the government was worried about celebrating the anniversary too ostentatiously. France was already considered with suspicion by the rest of monarchical Europe as a regicidal upstart, a hotbed of bloody republicanism. It would be best, some timorous officials concluded, to mark the centennial en famille and not disturb neighboring crowned heads with an international celebration of revolution. Besides, they suspected that invitations to exhibit at a world's fair held to commemorate 1789 might be met with rebuffs from the monarchies. Prime Minister Jules Ferry, an outspoken, energetic republican who as minister of education had made free secular schooling compulsory and as prime minister had been one of the chief promoters of France's colonial expansion, thought otherwise. He favored a world's fair as a vehicle for demonstrating France's newly recovered place in the sun, her industrial might, commercial activity and engineering skill. His view ultimately prevailed, and on November 8, 1884, President Grévy signed a brief decree ordering that "A Universal Exposition of the Products of Industry shall be opened in Paris May 5, 1889, and closed October 31 following." Neither Grévy nor even the audacious Ferry could foresee that this would be the largest, most varied and most spectacularly successful world's fair ever held until that time.*

The industrial fair was an invention of the nineteenth century, and therefore an especially apt form for the centennial of 1789. Paris and London had used such fairs throughout the century as showcases for their progress as they vied for first place in Europe. Occasionally the rivalry sharpened to reflect a state of heightened tension, as at France's fair in 1798, sponsored by the Directory while Napoleon's armies battled the British. "The participant who can show that his products and trade have dealt the worst blow to English industry will receive a gold medal,"

* Ferry's government fell five months later, and Grévy resigned in December 1887. In all, the great fair would be prepared by four successive governments, about par for the Third Republic.

6

the government promised. In general, however, the competition was more gentlemanly, in keeping with the cosmopolitan spirit of Europe's fairs dating back to the important ones of Champagne in the twelfth century, which brought together the best products from around the world: Flemish and English fabrics, German linens, Russian furs, spices from the Orient. The two annual fairs at Troyes, 100 miles east of Paris, assumed such importance that "troy weights" became a standard measure.

The first nation to enter the industrial era was also the first to hold an industrial world's fair, when Prince Albert invited all "civilized" nations to an exhibition that opened in Hyde Park on May 1, 1851. Over 13,000 participants responded, nearly half of them non-British. The fair's main attraction was Joseph Paxton's colossal Crystal Palace. An airy bubble of glass with iron ribs, the Palace had nearly one million square feet of floor space and was the largest enclosure yet constructed, prefiguring the innovative use of iron later in the century. The fair was seen by over six million visitors and set a standard for international exhibitions that followed.

France took up the gauntlet and inaugurated a series of world's fairs at roughly eleven-year intervals beginning in 1855 and reaching its climax in 1900. Although London never again mounted an exhibition to match the Crystal Palace, Paris progressed steadily from one brilliant success to another. Its first Palais de l'Industrie, a cathedral of commerce with a glass and iron central nave twice as wide as that of the Crystal Palace, gave notice in 1855 of things to come. An attendance record of fifteen million was set at the Paris fair of 1867. This figure rose slightly to sixteen million in 1878 and shot to over thirty-two million in 1889, as Victorian enthusiasm for the era's wondrous new machines grew apace.

The organizers of the Paris Exposition of 1889 soft-pedaled its role as the centennial celebration of the French Revolution out of consideration for aristocratic sensibilities both at home and abroad. (In France itself the Republic was still contemptuously called *la gueuse* by monarchists, and titled residents defiantly shuttered their windows every July 14.) Political implications were de-emphasized in the prospectus prepared in March 1885 by the government study committee. "The Exposition of 1889," it stated, "will have the character of a centennial exhibit, summing up what freedom of work has produced in terms of progress during the past hundred years. 1789 was a historic date in economics as well as politics, and it is to examine the world's economic situation that all nations are invited."

All nations were not entirely convinced that the basic significance of France's centennial was economic, however, and several monarchies, including Austria-Hungary, Belgium, Britain and Holland refused official participation in the fair. Their exhibits eventually were organized by private interests. Germany, reflecting the continuing tension with a France dedicated to regaining Alsace and Lorraine, remained pointedly aloof.

With governmental instability hampering plans for the fair — Ferry's replacement as prime minister, Henri Brisson, lasted only nine months — the project did not really begin taking shape until the spring of 1886, only three years before the official opening date. A second wind was provided in good part by the new minister of commerce and industry, Edouard Lockroy, one of the more original cabinet members to serve the Third Republic. A graduate of the Beaux-Arts, author of several comedies and operettas, sometime journalist, Lockroy was a littérateur who moved in the same circles as Victor Hugo and was known for his biting wit. The centennial exposition caught his fancy, and he pushed through its budget of $8.6 million to be provided by the government, the City of Paris and a private company founded to underwrite the fair. It was also Lockroy who, casting about for an appropriate, Babel-like symbol for the fair, took up and promoted the idea of a thousand-foot tower.

Edouard Lockroy, minister of commerce and industry, was in charge of initial plans for the Paris Universal Exposition of 1889.

The notion itself was not particularly new. In fact, it was in the air on both sides of the Atlantic as the nations that had been the first to realize the early potential of the Industrial Revolution looked for ways to dramatize their new prowess and prosperity. It was as if they were obeying a compulsion constant throughout history to thrust mighty structures toward the sky in moments of special pride: in legend the Tower of Babel, in reality the Great Pyramid of Cheops and the medieval cathedrals.

The difference in the nineteenth century was that whereas the pretext, at least, for such previous exercises nearly always had been religious, the new secular faith in material progress justified an engineering feat for its own sake. Actually, 1889 marked the centenary of what a British historian, E. J. Hobsbawm, has called the Dual Revolution that transformed Europe: the French Revolution, which provided the seminal political and social ideology for the Western world, and the Industrial Revolution, which seemingly furnished the means to attain liberty, equality and

9

fraternity. Confidence in progress and human perfectibility then was at a peak that from the postindustrial perspective appears touchingly naive. As Georges Berger, the ebullient general manager of the Exposition of 1889, expressed its goal:

> We will show our sons what their fathers have accomplished in the space of a century through progress in knowledge, love of work and respect for liberty. We will give them a view from the summit of the steep slope that has been climbed since the dark ages. And if one day they should again descend to some valley of error and misery, they will remember what we did and they will remind their children of it, and future generations will thereby be more determined than ever to climb still higher than we have. For the law of progress is immortal, just as progress itself is infinite.

As early as March 1833, the great British railroad engineer Richard Trevithick had proposed a thousand-foot tower for London to commemorate passage of the First Reform Act. The structure was to have been of cast iron, 100 feet in diameter at the base and ten feet across at the top, surmounted by a colossal statue. Trevithick died in April of that year, however, and his idea was not acted upon by King William IV. Later, in 1874, two American engineers, Clarke and Reeves, drew up plans for a thousand-foot tower of iron for the Philadelphia Centennial Exposition of 1876. The cylinder was to be only thirty feet in diameter, braced by cables attached to a circular masonry base. The exposition's organizers rejected what must have resembled a glorified factory chimney. The most ambitious tower actually to be erected before 1889 was the Washington Monument. But this 555-foot, all-masonry structure completed in 1884 was far smaller than the thousand-foot tower that had become a virtual obsession of nineteenth-century engineers.

Therefore when Edouard Lockroy considered how to give the Paris Exposition of 1889 special éclat, a thousand-foot tower was

10

an obvious choice. In the notice published in the government's *Journal Officiel* of May 2, 1886, French architects and engineers bidding to construct the fair's semipermanent buildings and other attractions were invited to "study the possibility of erecting on the Champ de Mars an iron tower with a base 125 meters square and 300 meters high.* If they consider it desirable they may present a different plan without such a tower." Despite the admissibility of designs omitting a tower, it was clear that Lockroy wanted one.

With time running short, contestants had only sixteen days in which to draw up their initial blueprints. Over 100 projects came in by the May 18 deadline. The projects were shown to the public for three days and considered by Lockroy's Exposition committee for five days before winners of the twelve prizes, ranging from $800 to $200, were announced. Working hastily, the committee rejected out of hand dozens of perfervidly inventive projects. One designer, for example, proposed a tower in the form of a gigantic garden sprinkler which could be used, he claimed, to water Paris in case of drought. Another envisioned an immense guillotine to symbolize the Revolution. One apparently valid idea by Nachon-Cassien was a tower bestriding the Seine at the Pont d'Iéna, linking the Champ de Mars and the Trocadéro gardens. This plan was finally disqualified because of the danger of laying foundations for a tower of several thousand tons directly on the riverbed; besides, official criteria required that the tower be on the Champ de Mars itself.

Another intriguing proposal, by two engineers named Bourdais and Sébillot, described a thousand-foot tower with a powerful electric light at its summit. A system of parabolic mirrors would reflect light so efficiently from the tower at its proposed site on the Esplanade des Invalides to all parts of Paris that even the most remote quarters of the city would receive, as the engineers con-

* Three hundred meters, or 986 feet, was the nearest round metric equivalent to a thousand feet.

Gustave Eiffel in 1889.

fidently put it, "eight times as much light as is necessary to read a newspaper." Night would be banished from the City of Light. Moreover, the all-granite "Tour Soleil" would be composed of six levels with fifteen rooms on each, to be used for "aerotherapy treatments" where the sick would benefit from air as pure as that in the Alps. The tower's hollow center would allow for scientific experiments involving falling objects, and a basement 215 feet deep would house a multistory museum dedicated to electricity. The structure was to be topped off by a 180-foot allegorical statue representing Science.

If Lockroy's committee finally selected Gustave Eiffel's proposal for a tower of iron weighing approximately 7000 tons and costing $1.6 million, it was partly because of Eiffel's unequaled prestige at fifty-three years of age as France's master builder in metal, partly because his project was the most practicable in light of official criteria — but mainly because those criteria were established with Eiffel's design specifically in mind.

His project had in fact been on paper since the latter part of 1884. Prompted by official talk of the Exposition of 1889,

13

Left: *A sampling of thousand-foot towers proposed for the Exposition.*

Maurice Koechlin, Eiffel's chief of research at Eiffel and Company, in cooperation with another engineer, Emile Nouguier, and the company's architect, Stephen Sauvestre, began initial studies for a tower in June of that year. Koechlin, a Swiss-naturalized Alsatian who had graduated from the prestigious Federal Polytechnic School in Zurich, actually designed the Eiffel Tower. This fact has occasionally stirred up teapot tempests, mainly in Swiss newspapers, over whether Eiffel stole the idea for the tower from Koechlin. As it happened, Eiffel always gave full credit to Koechlin for the part he played in the initial conception of the tower, and in later life Koechlin never claimed more in the speeches he made on the subject. The project was a company effort; the research bureau turned out several versions of a thousand-foot tower and Eiffel chose the one he considered most likely, assuming full responsibility for its execution.

Eiffel's project first became public in December 1884, when it was outlined in a French civil engineering review and in a daily newspaper, *La France*. The following May, Eiffel mentioned the proposal in an address to the French Society of Civil Engineers. Shortly afterward, Eiffel called on Lockroy and presented the tower as a centerpiece for the Exposition of 1889. His success in selling the idea can be seen in the criteria later laid down by Lockroy, who formulated them along the lines of Eiffel's proposal, including a base precisely 125 meters square.

Moreover, while the competition was still going on, Lockroy named a subcommittee on May 12 to study the technical feasibility of Eiffel's iron structure. When the group met on June 12, the die was, in effect, cast. "The subcommittee rejected several projects as unrealistic," notes the official history of the Exposition of 1889, "several others as insufficiently thorough, and finally decided unanimously that the tower to be erected at the Universal Exposition of 1889 should have a well-defined character and appear as an original masterpiece of the metals industry, and that only the Eiffel Tower seemed to fulfill these requirements." The

Eiffel's project as presented to the Exposition committee.

subcommittee recommended adoption of Eiffel's proposal, on condition that further study be given to the particularly complex questions of the tower's elevators and protection from lightning.

Eiffel, an energetic entrepreneur, had stolen a march on the competition by getting to Lockroy first, but he had also presented a compelling case, demolishing in the process the notion that a thousand-foot tower could be built of masonry. A stone tower of such height, he argued, would present special problems concerning settling of its foundations, cohesion of mortar under unprecedented pressures and the construction time required if traditional methods were used. Building in stone had reached the limit of its technology: "Antiquity, the Middle Ages and the Renaissance have pushed the use of stone to the extreme," he reasoned, "and it hardly appears possible to go further than our predecessors have with the same materials, especially since masonry construction techniques have not progressed notably for some time." He pointed out that the world's tallest stone structure, the Washington Monument, was only 555 feet high, and the age's other monuments, particularly Europe's soaring cathedral spires, were still smaller: Cologne Cathedral, for instance, reached only 512 feet, Rouen was 492 feet and Chartres 370 feet. Saint Paul's dome in London rose 361 feet, and the dome of Washington's Capitol was 305 feet high. Clearly, new ambitions called for new materials and techniques previously unavailable.

That meant cast iron, wrought iron or steel, the metals that had revolutionized construction in the nineteenth century, enabling engineers to meet the demands of the railroads for hundreds of bridges, train sheds and other infrastructure. Cast iron, brittle and lacking tensile strength, was suitable only in the same compressive role as stone, for columns and arches. Steel, on the other hand, was lighter and more flexible, perhaps too much so for the tower Eiffel had in mind; he feared that steel's greater elasticity would produce an intolerable amount of sway in high winds. Steel also was considerably more costly, since it was just then coming into mass production. Thus his project was a wrought-iron structure that would combine strength with rigidity and still be relatively light. Moreover, Eiffel held out the possibility of dismantling his iron tower if the City of Paris so desired at a later date, an option administrators would not have with a masonry structure.

Eiffel's authoritative arguments were buttressed by his long experience in iron construction. He had been building railway bridges and a host of other metal structures in France and abroad for thirty years. He now claimed to have devised a system of lattice-trussed piers with incurving edges that theoretically made it possible to construct towers of any height. The Exposition committee was willing to gamble that his new system would work.

On January 8, 1887, seven months after the Exposition's sub-committee voted in favor of Eiffel's proposal, Edouard Lockroy and the City of Paris signed a contract with Eiffel. The engineer agreed to construct a thousand-foot tower corresponding to his proposal in time for the opening of the Exposition of 1889. He was to receive a subsidy of $300,000 in three installments, the last due on the date of completion, and was given a franchise to operate the tower and to open restaurants, cafés and other attractions on it during the Exposition and for the following twenty years, after which full ownership would return to the City of Paris.

To anyone but the supremely confident Eiffel, the undertaking would have appeared foolhardy, questions of the basic wisdom of creating such an eccentric structure aside. For one thing, the Exposition committee had procrastinated to the point where a scant two years remained in which to construct the tallest tower ever conceived, for which no guiding precedent existed. The Washington Monument had taken thirty-six years from corner-stone to capstone, including time lost due to financial and technical problems. Moreover, the subsidy granted by the French government covered less than one-fifth of the tower's projected

*The four piers begin to rise, July 1887. In background is
the Trocadéro Palace.*

cost. Eiffel was to provide the remainder, $1.3 million, with the
possibility of recovering his investment if the tower turned out a
financial success.

But there was no question now of turning back. France had announced to the world the most complete, the most dazzling international exposition ever held, the hallmark of which would be the
thousand-foot tower that seemed the inevitable technical apotheo-
sis of the century.

For three more weeks the Exposition committee indulged its
proclivity for dither while it considered where, exactly, the tower
should stand. Members wondered whether the initial choice of
location at the end of the Champ de Mars near the Seine might
not spoil the area's proportions. Perhaps the tower would be set
off to advantage by being placed atop Mont Valérien, a few miles
to the west, rather than at a low point near the river. Or perhaps

such a distinctive monument installed permanently in the area would intrude on subsequent fairs with different architecture and layout. Financial considerations finally dictated that the tower be close enough to the fairgrounds that both the fair and the tower would benefit from their combined appeal to the public. Also, on the Champ de Mars the tower's gigantic arches would have the additional role of monumental entrance to the fair, saving the government the cost of constructing one.

The final decision made, workers began digging the tower's foundations on January 26. There was never any doubt in Eiffel's mind that he was engaged in a historic enterprise. It was his intention, he said, "to raise to the glory of modern science, and to the greater honor of French industry, an arch of triumph as striking as those that preceding generations had raised to conquerors." The tower's immediate symbolic importance for France

19

and, in particular, for the Exposition of 1889, was spelled out by Alfred Picard, official historian of the Exposition: "This colossal work was to constitute a brilliant manifestation of the industrial strength of our country, attest to the immense progress realized in the art of metal structures, celebrate the unprecedented progress of civil engineering during the course of this century, attract multitudes of visitors and contribute largely to the success of the great peaceful commemoration of the centenary of 1789." Eventually, and not altogether incidentally, the tower was also to make a great deal of money.

But before that, even before its construction had got well under way, the tower was to make a number of people angry. Paris had been talking for months of Eiffel's project, mostly with the boulevardier's amused skepticism. When the first cubic yards of earth began to leave the Champ de Mars, however, it became clear that the thing would actually be attempted. The technical feasibility of a thousand-foot tower escaped most Parisians' judgment, but its potential effect on the city's skyline did not. Self-appointed tastemakers in this nation that prided itself on being beauty's most devoted acolyte rose up in rage. Forty-seven of the most righteously indignant penned a letter of protest in early February to Charles Adolphe Alphand, the minister of public works, who was responsible within the government for the Exposition. Redolent of its time and place, the *protestation des artistes* is worth savoring in full:

> Writers, painters, sculptors, architects, passionate lovers of the heretofore intact beauty of Paris, we come to protest with all our strength, with all our indignation, in the name of betrayed French taste, in the name of threatened French art and history, against the erection in the heart of our capital of the useless and monstrous Eiffel Tower, which the public has scornfully and rightly dubbed the Tower of Babel.
>
> Without being blind chauvinists, we have the right to proclaim publicly that Paris is without rival in the world. Along its streets

20

and wide boulevards, beside its admirable riverbanks, amid its magnificent promenades, stand the most noble monuments to which human genius has ever given birth. The soul of France, the creator of masterpieces, shines among this august proliferation of stone. Italy, Germany, Flanders, so rightly proud of their artistic heritage, possess nothing comparable to ours, and Paris attracts curiosity and admiration from all corners of the universe. Are we to let all that be profaned? Is the City of Paris to associate itself any longer with the baroque, mercantile imaginings of a builder of machines, and thus dishonor and disfigure itself irreparably? For the Eiffel Tower, which even commercial America would not have, is without a doubt the dishonor of Paris. Everyone feels it, everyone says it, everyone is profoundly saddened by it, and we are only a weak echo of public opinion so legitimately alarmed. When foreigners visit our Exposition they will cry out in astonishment, "Is it this horror that the French have created to give us an idea of their vaunted taste?" They will be right to mock us, for the Paris of sublime gothic, the Paris of Jean Goujon, of Germain Pilon, of Puget, of Rude, of Barye, etc., will have become the Paris of Monsieur Eiffel.

For that matter, all one must do to understand our case is to imagine for a moment a dizzily ridiculous tower dominating Paris like a black and gigantic factory chimney, crushing beneath its barbarous mass Notre Dame, the Sainte Chapelle, the Tour Saint Jacques, the Louvre, the dome of the Invalides, the Arc de Triomphe, all our humiliated monuments, all our raped architecture disappearing in this stupefying dream. And for the next twenty years we will see cast over the entire city, still trembling with the genius of so many centuries, cast like a spot of ink, the odious shadow of the odious column of bolted metal.

It is up to you who so love Paris, who have so beautified it, who have so often protected it against administrative devastation and the vandalism of industry, to defend it once again. We entrust to you the task of pleading the cause of Paris, knowing that you will bring to it all the energy, all the eloquence that the love of the beautiful, the great, the proper inspire in an artist as your-

21

self. And if our cry of alarm is not heard, if our argument is not listened to, if Paris stubbornly goes ahead with an idea that dishonors Paris, we will at least, you and we, have expressed an honorable protest.

The letter was signed by Ernest Meissonier, the painter, Charles Gounod, composer of *Faust*, Charles Garnier, architect of the Paris Opéra, Adolphe William Bouguereau, a leading painter of the pompous "academic" school, such writers as Alexandre Dumas fils, François Coppée, Leconte de Lisle, Sully Prudhomme and Guy de Maupassant, and three dozen lesser lights. Their outrage was typical of the snobbish attitude still prevalent today toward anything that dares be as sheerly *obvious* as the Eiffel Tower. The writers, especially, continued to heap scorn upon it, unaware that it would become a semisacred object of contemplation for a later generation of writers. Maupassant in particular professed boundless contempt for the structure. The probably apocryphal story is still told in Paris that he frequently lunched at the restaurant on the second platform because that was the only place in the city where he could be certain not to see the tower. In his short story *"La Vie Errante,"* he declares:

I left Paris and even France because of the Eiffel Tower. Not only is it visible from every point in the city, but it is to be found everywhere, made of every known material, exhibited in every shop window, an unavoidable and tormenting nightmare . . . I wonder what will be thought of our generation if, in some future riot, we do not unbolt this tall, skinny pyramid of iron ladders, this giant and disgraceful skeleton with a base that seems made to support a formidable monument of Cyclops and which aborts into the thin, ridiculous profile of a factory chimney.

He was joined in his dudgeon notably by the morose Léon Bloy, who called the tower "a superb hardware shop," and wrote darkly, "I love Paris, the city of intelligence, and I feel Paris threatened by this truly tragic lamppost to which it has given birth and which will be seen at night from twenty leagues . . .

22

as a distress signal of shipwreck and despair." Despair in this case was in the eye of the beholder, judging by the enthusiastic response to the tower elsewhere, but Bloy's view was characteristic enough of a certain segment of the population. As the poet Léon-Paul Fargue, who happened to like the tower, put it later, "when [the tower] came shooting out of the earth, the aesthetes liked it not at all." But this was long before the tower's appeal to the masses led the French National Tourist Office to plead in full-color advertisements, "Do we have to put an Eiffel Tower in every town to get you to appreciate the rest of France?"

Alphand passed the letter on to Lockroy, for whom it was a rare and obviously delightful opportunity to exercise his ironic pen. Ostensibly replying to Alphand but fully expecting his note to get to the Paris papers, Lockroy wrote:

Judging by the stately swell of the rhythms, the beauty of the metaphors, the elegance of its delicate and precise style, one can tell without even looking at the signatures that this protest is the result of collaboration of the most famous writers and poets of our time . . . But do not let yourself be impressed by its beautiful form, and note only the facts. The protest is already irrelevant. You will inform the senders that construction of the tower was decided upon a year ago and that the work site has been open for a month. They could have protested in time: they did not, and "honorable" indignation unfortunately comes a bit late.

I am profoundly sorry about this. Not that I fear for Paris. Notre Dame will remain Notre Dame and the Arc de Triomphe will remain the Arc de Triomphe. But I could have saved the only part of this great city which is seriously in danger: that incomparable sand pile called the Champ de Mars, such an inspiration for our poets and so attractive to our landscape painters.

Please express my sorrow to these gentlemen. Above all do not say that it is unfortunate that the Exposition is being attacked by those who should be defending it; that a protest signed by such illustrious names will echo throughout Europe and may be used as a pretext by some nations not to take part in our celebration;

that it is bad to attempt to ridicule a peaceful undertaking that France is so attached to, especially now when she is so unjustly suspected abroad. Such petty considerations concern a cabinet minister, but they are meaningless for rarefied minds which are occupied above all with the interests of art and the love of the beautiful.

What I pray you to do is to accept this protest and to keep it. It should be placed in a showcase at the Exposition. Such beautiful and noble prose cannot but interest the crowds, and perhaps even amaze them.

Lockroy's sarcasm was the perfect parry to the little band of overzealous keepers of the Grail, subjecting them to the one thing they could not stand, public ridicule. They were not heard from again, and several came to be open admirers of the tower.

Before this quintessentially French *affaire* was over, the tower's creator had his say on the subject — an unusual event in an era when engineers were most often considered boors whose aesthetic notions scarcely went beyond the beauty of a neatly placed rivet. In fact, many engineers of the time were simple mechanics of little education, such as James Watt and Thomas Newcomen, whose steam engines were the motive force of the Industrial Revolution. Richard Trevithick had been a carnival strong man and wrestler before trying his hand at locomotives. And Herbert Hoover recalled that in his younger days he had given a nasty shock to an English lady, who shared his table during a trans-Atlantic crossing, by admitting that he was a mining engineer.

Eiffel, however, was a graduate of France's rigorous lycée system as well as of its proud Ecole Centrale des Arts et Manufactures, one of Europe's first great engineering schools. His sketchbooks filled with pencil drawings indicate a highly cultivated sensibility. As to the hostile reaction by part of the artist community to his tower, Eiffel viewed the matter with solid Burgundian equanimity and a sure grasp of aesthetics. "I believe

24

that the tower will have its own beauty," he declared in an interview published in the serious daily, *Le Temps*. "The first principle of architectural beauty is that the essential lines of a construction be determined by a perfect appropriateness to its use. What was the main obstacle I had to overcome in designing the tower? Its resistance to wind. And I submit that the curves of its four piers as produced by our calculations, rising from an enormous base and narrowing toward the top, will give a great impression of strength and beauty." Clearly, the idea that form follows function was not exclusive to the Chicago School of architecture, which was beginning to apply it to the world's first skyscrapers. Interestingly enough in this case, an engineer, not an architect, had articulated the concept. But then Louis Sullivan himself concluded that the most exciting and original advances of his time in building technique were the work of engineers rather than architects.

"Besides," Eiffel continued, on another tack, "there is an attraction and a charm inherent in the colossal that is not subject to ordinary theories of art. Does anyone pretend that the Pyramids have so forcefully gripped the imagination of men through their artistic value? What are they after all but artificial hillocks? And yet what visitor can stand without reaction in their presence? The tower will be the tallest edifice ever raised by man. Will it not therefore be imposing in its own way?" He concluded on the note that had come to be the leitmotif of the Exposition of 1889, France's emotional need to be taken seriously in the community of nations. "It seems to me that the Eiffel Tower is worthy of being treated with respect, if only because it will show that we are not simply an amusing people, but also the country of engineers and builders who are called upon all over the world to construct bridges, viaducts, train stations and the great monuments of modern industry."

France had come a long way since its humiliation in 1870, and it intended to prove it to a skeptical world — and coincidentally to itself — with the Exposition of 1889 and a tower so tall that other nations had only dreamed of such a monument. The country was riding the crest of the first wave of industrialism. In a broader sense, the iron tower that was to symbolize France's soaring pride of accomplishment would also signal that a new era, full of incalculable portent, had begun.

TWO

THE INDUSTRIAL AGE, which Gustave Eiffel exemplified in his career and celebrated with his tower, was just fifty years old when he was born. Such a statement admittedly is possible only through a willing suspension of disbelief in the distinctness of historical eras. In this case, historians seem to agree that the Industrial Revolution "occurred" in Great Britain in the 1780s. While there had been in history previous periods of great creativity, bustle and relative prosperity, it was during that decade that, thanks to radically new developments in work organization and power production, Britain "took off" into the continuous self-sustained growth that characterizes an industrial economy. Other European nations and the United States, informed by the liberating rationalist thought of the eighteenth-century Enlightenment and poised economically on the verge of takeoff, soon followed. By the 1820s sociologists in Britain and France actually had coined the term Industrial Revolution, and there was a spurt of other neologisms to take into account new social and economic realities: industrialist, engineer, factory and railway were either entirely new notions or evolved significantly during this period.

Perhaps not the least peculiar aspect of the era was that this particular revolution was effected not by generals or politicians but by engineers. This cloddish and often despised class mined the coal, designed the blast furnaces and steam engines, laid out railway lines and flung bridges by the score across rivers and gorges and, in sum, provided the infrastructure on which the new and, it was hoped, universal prosperity was to stand. "These are indeed glorious times for the Engineers," exulted James Nasmyth, the Scottish inventor who designed the first steam hammer. His mood was echoed throughout the industrializing world. The engineer of the early industrial age was a pragmatic sort, generally uneducated in the classical sense, but his ability to cope with problems posed by the new technology earned him increasing appreciation. "If we want any work done of an unusual character and send for an architect," Prince Albert was said to have observed, "he hesitates, debates, trifles; we send for an engineer, and he *does it*." As the century advanced and their profession was put on a more scientific basis, engineers were to realize monumental works with the functional beauty of perfectly resolved mathematical equations.

Perhaps inevitably, their accomplishments often were unappreciated at the time; less pardonably, they are in many cases underappreciated still, despite their historical uniqueness and their contributions to the fund of knowledge of how to get things done. As James Marston Fitch, professor of architecture at Columbia University, points out, "The nineteenth century saw three great developments in structural theory: the enclosure of great areas in the Crystal Palace; the spanning of great voids in the Brooklyn Bridge; and the reaching of great heights in the Eiffel Tower . . . Each of these structures was, in a way, the product of a golden moment of equilibrium, brief in time, special in character, delicate in balance. Their significance was dissipated before men of adequate stature could again appear to grasp it."

Besides being the work of engineers, these three landmark creations had another significant point in common: the imaginative and resourceful use of iron.

A banal metal utilized for over 3000 years for limited produc-

28

tion of tools and weapons, iron had always been valued for its hardness and strength. The number of uses it could be put to was limited by the state of technology, however, and local smithies generally were able to satisfy demand from their simple forges until well into the eighteenth century. With the coming of the Industrial Revolution, iron's qualities were rediscovered in the light of new needs, and its rapidly growing use virtually transformed the early industrial era into a second Iron Age. If a single development could be pinpointed as the most important in the concatenation of causes that sparked the Industrial Revolution, it might well be the discovery around 1709 by an English iron master, Abraham Darby, that iron could be smelted with coke, made from plentiful coal, rather than with charcoal.

With the help of bigger blast furnaces and more sophisticated metallurgical techniques, iron production made exponential leaps during the nineteenth century. World output of pig iron, estimated at one million tons in 1820, grew to 39.8 million in 1900. Strong as stone in compression but far more resistant to shear and tension, iron freed civil engineers from the arch, the vault and the dome. For the first time since Alberti had formulated the principles of masonry construction in the late fifteenth century, builders could take an entirely new approach — based on intelligent economy rather than sheer mass — to structural problems. The result was what one architectural historian, Carl Condit of the University of Chicago, has called "The most profound and far-reaching revolution in the history of the building arts."

Builders' habits were not always easily changed, however. Paris' central market, Les Halles, was originally conceived in classical masonry in 1851 by Victor Baltard, an assiduous student of Greek and Roman ruins. Emperor Napoleon III, in an unwonted access of modernism, was furious when he saw the structure and had it torn down. Calling in the prefect of Paris, Baron Eugène Haussmann, the emperor decreed that the market should resemble "big umbrellas." Haussmann, who created modern Paris by cutting great swaths — today's boulevards —

through the jumbled city, urged Baltard to use iron. Baltard went back to his drawing board and created the twelve soaring glass and iron pavilions on slim cast-iron columns that caught and delighted the eye from 1867 until they were demolished in 1971. Emile Zola called them the only original monument constructed in France during the nineteenth century; later, Mies van der Rohe termed Les Halles "the symbol of the golden age of French building techniques." The end products of those techniques were the Eiffel Tower and the American skyscraper.

Indeed, there is an intriguing link between the tower and the first true skyscraper, Chicago's Home Insurance Building. Completed in 1885, four years before the Eiffel Tower, the Home Insurance Building was designed with interior iron framing, reducing the walls to nothing more than the protective envelope that characterizes the glass-walled skyscrapers of today. Its architect, William Le Baron Jenney, drew much of his knowledge of modern iron-framing techniques from his studies in France. Before going to Chicago to become the mentor of many of the brilliant young architects of the Chicago School, such as Louis Sullivan, William Holabird and Martin Roche, Jenney spent three years in Paris at the Ecole Centrale des Arts et Manufactures, graduating in 1856, a year after his schoolmate, Gustave Eiffel.

The irony — if the term is not outrageous in this context — of Eiffel's career is that the man whom the French proclaim *"Le Magicien du Fer"* knew little about metal construction when he left the Ecole Centrale at age twenty-two. He had in fact studied chemical engineering and aspired to nothing more than a job at an uncle's vinegar distillery in his home town of Dijon. A conventional, rather prim, most Victorian young man, Eiffel was disappointed at the turn of events that upset his comfortable plans to become a maker of fine vinegar, but he gamely took a job as factotum to the head of a Paris construction firm specializing in railway equipment. The direction of Eiffel's career was thus initially decided by luck. Although aloof and formal by nature, he appears to have retained a charming modesty until his death at ninety-one, and his references to the tower that made him world famous were nearly always marked with mild self-astonishment. But fate was to lend a Sophoclean touch to the life of this basically simple man, dealing Eiffel a blow in a moment of seeming hubris from which he never fully recovered and which cast an unfortunate and unfair shadow over his reputation in France.

Alexandre Gustave Boenickhausen-Eiffel was the great-great-grandson of Jean-René Boenickhausen, who emigrated to France from a village near Cologne in the early eighteenth century and became a forester. (The builder of the tower was the third of a trio of men of Rhenish origin who shaped the face of Paris in the nineteenth century; the other two were the engineer Jacques Hittorf, who designed the Champs Elysées and the Place de la Concorde, and Eugène Haussmann.) Jean-René's principal achievement, for our purposes, was to assume the name Eiffel, derived from the Eifel plateau region of his birth, so that he might appear less of a foreigner.* His son Jean-Pierre Henri married the daughter of a prosperous Paris tapestry merchant and became a *maître-tapissier* himself when tapestry making was one of the elite crafts of France. The trade was passed on from father to son for two generations, until Gustave Eiffel's father, François Alexandre, broke the pattern in favor of military adventure by joining Napoleon's Imperial Army at age sixteen in 1811. Wounded twice with the Fifth Hussar Regiment of Berchiny during the Italian campaign, François Alexandre was posted to the garrison at Dijon after Waterloo and there met and married Catherine-Mélanie Moneuse, the daughter of a lumber merchant. The first of three children and only son, Alexandre Gustave was born in Dijon on December 15, 1832.

In his brief memoirs Gustave Eiffel devotes many pages to a

* Boenickhausen-Eiffel remained the legal family name until December 1880, when a court in Dijon, acting on Gustave Eiffel's request, officially authorized the deletion of Boenickhausen.

31

François Alexandre Eiffel.

Catherine-Mélanie Eiffel.

Gustave Eiffel at 18.

fond description of his childhood in Dijon. Surprisingly for a man of his practical turn of mind, Eiffel, when he was ninety, wrote that he remembered those tender years better than any other period of his life. It was an ordinary, happy, provincial childhood, punctuated by occasional raps on the knuckles and Sunday visits to the neighborhood patisserie. Good republican principles were inculcated by Uncle Jean-Baptiste Mollerat, a chemist who had invented a process for distilling vinegar from wood, and who enjoyed locally the reputation of having seen Robespierre guillotined. He frequently reminded the impressionable youngster that "all kings are rascals," driving home the point with a stern look, through glittering pince-nez, that Eiffel never forgot.

Learning was a distasteful, rote process at the prisonlike Lycée Royal, and Gustave was an indifferent pupil until his last years there, when two sympathetic teachers awakened his interest in history and literature. He managed the difficult achievement of passing a double *baccalaureat* in literature and science, and was sent to the elite Collège Sainte Barbe in Paris in preparation for the Polytechnique. The capital was a stimulant to the young provincial, and despite the strict Victorian discipline of Sainte Barbe he found time to discover the joys of the quadrille and to meet his first English girls. "They're lots of fun," he wrote home, to the probable consternation of his parents. "Much less reserved than French girls."

Due to a slip during a final exam, Eiffel failed in the summer of 1852 to gain entrance to the Polytechnique, the most prestigious school in France and the goal of all good bourgeois families for their sons. Founded in 1795, the Polytechnique — imitated in Germany and Belgium, and from Zurich to Vienna and Prague to Saint Petersburg — was in large part responsible for France's supremacy in maths and science during much of the nineteenth century. His failure to enter there seems to have disappointed his parents more than Eiffel, who never admitted to grand ambitions or underestimated his real value. Without missing a beat he opted for the Ecole Centrale des Arts et Manufactures, an institution not the less estimable for lacking the Polytechnique's luster. Unlike the state-run, semimilitary Polytechnique, whose superbly trained and disciplined graduates usually went on to government service, the Ecole Centrale was a more liberal private school that graduated solid, self-reliant technicians and engineers.

Eiffel chose chemistry as his major field of study, for he had been given to understand that upon graduation he would have a place at his Uncle Mollerat's vinegar firm in Dijon. Just before he took his degree in 1855, however, the Eiffel and Mollerat families ceased speaking to each other as the result of a trivial but violent political quarrel. Under the circumstances there was no question of the young graduate's joining his uncle, so he rounded up several letters of recommendation and began looking for a job in Paris.

As a graduate of Centrale, he was welcomed by Charles Nepveu, an official in the French Society of Civil Engineers, whose firm specialized in the construction of steam engines, rolling stock and other railway equipment. Nepveu offered a salary of $30 per month and the opportunity to learn the business, and Eiffel gladly took the job of personal secretary and man Friday. The arrangement lasted only a few months, for the high-strung Nepveu was a better engineer than businessman and his company shortly went bankrupt while he had a nervous breakdown. He and his young protégé managed to land on their feet, thanks to a big Belgian railway equipment firm that merged with Nepveu to form the General Railway Equipment Company. Nepveu became director of the company's Paris office, with Eiffel as chief of research — at $50 per month.

Eiffel's providential knock at Nepveu's door put him on the ground floor of the fastest growing, most dynamic industry of the industrious nineteenth century. The railway was, literally, the

The bridge across the Garonne at Bordeaux, completed in 1855.

vehicle of the Industrial Revolution. Not only did it provide a reliable, low-cost, high-volume system of land transportation, it also served as an outlet for capital investment, created employment and stimulated the coal and iron industries. Railway requirements encouraged research into steam power and new approaches to architectural engineering for bridge and train shed construction. For nearly half a century this was the predominant business of the industrializing world.

After Britain opened the Stockton-Darlington line in 1825, the world's first public railway for freight and passengers, other state railways followed in France in 1828, Germany and Austria in 1835, and the rush was on. During the peak of Britain's "railway mania" in the 1840s Parliament authorized construction of over 400 railways. France's network was rather late-blooming, but by the time Gustave Eiffel fortuitously abandoned chemistry for civil engineering, French railway construction was at its height — nearly 8000 miles of track were laid from 1852 to 1857 — and six main companies had been formed.

Eiffel's first big job, at twenty-five, was commissioned by two of those lines, the Compagnie d'Orléans and the Compagnie du Midi, which decided in 1858 to join their networks with a bridge across the Garonne River at Bordeaux. Eiffel was charged with overseeing the whole $600,000 operation and insuring that the June 1860 deadline was met.

Two years was a short time in which to build a 1600-foot cast-iron railway bridge on six piers across the turbulent Garonne. Eiffel, working sixteen-hour days, boldly decided to use a time-saving new system of pile driving he had had the occasion to study when he began with Nepveu, but which had never been fully developed. The method, involving hydraulic presses and compressed air to sink the piles, worked as well in the eighty-foot-deep river as it had on paper. The structure opened on time as one of the largest iron bridges of the day, and Eiffel had begun to establish himself as an innovative engineer. He had also set the pattern that was to characterize his projects for the rest of his career: textbook execution of a carefully conceived, theoretically sound plan that freed him from the trial-and-error methods still prevalent in most engineering of the time, especially in England and the United States.

At Bordeaux only one incident appears to have upset Eiffel's precise calculations. A riveter fell into the Garonne one afternoon following a winy lunch, and was caught in the current. A strong swimmer who had won a bet when he was twenty by swimming the Seine at night, Eiffel removed his shoes and ever-present redingote, plunged in and saved the man. "Please be good enough to attach yourselves carefully in the future," he is said to have admonished the workers as he decorously buttoned the redingote over his dripping shirt and trousers. When the job was completed, the workers chipped in to have a medal designed showing the bridge and the hydraulic pile driver and presented it to Eiffel as a token of their esteem.

THREE

His CAREER STARTED, Eiffel began to long for domesticity. It was not satisfactory after all to post his shirts and underclothes to Dijon every week for washing and ironing. "What I need," he wrote his mother, "is a good housekeeper who won't get on my nerves too much, who will be as faithful as possible, and who will give me fine children." He was convinced that Dijon was the only proper place to find a wife, perhaps because of an unhappy affair in Bordeaux that finally required financial consolation for the lady in question. As it happened, a business associate of Eiffel père had a marriageable granddaughter who fit the description and possessed a dowry that met the pretensions of a rising young engineer. Eiffel had in fact known Marie Gaudelet since childhood; they were married in 1862 and set up in a comfortable apartment in Paris. They had five children before Marie's untimely death, probably of pneumonia, fifteen years later, when she was only thirty-two. Eiffel never remarried.

With the General Railway Equipment Company feeling the effects of a French recession, Eiffel left in 1864 and began freelancing as a consulting engineer. A job involving delivery of a consignment of locomotives to Egypt gave him the opportunity to

Eiffel with his wife, Marie, and their five children, 1877.

visit the recently opened Suez Canal. His observations there were
to prove useful years later when the builder of Suez, Ferdinand
de Lesseps, proposed a similar canal, without locks, across the
isthmus of Panama.

By 1867, Eiffel had opened his own metal-working shops in
Levallois-Perret, an industrial suburb northwest of Paris, and
was awarded a contract to design the iron arch-girders of the
Palais des Machines for the Paris Universal Exposition of that
year. During this machine-proud era, the machinery hall was
usually the most important building at a world's fair. Though
the machinery hall of 1867 would be surpassed at later fairs, it
was the largest until that time, an iron-framed ellipse 1608 by
1266 feet, its arches reaching a height of eighty-two feet.

In designing the arches, Eiffel once again decided against the
trial-and-error method of engineering and undertook to deter-

38

The Eiffels' home, "Le Castel," in Dijon.

Sketch by Eiffel of one of his country houses, "La Chaumière des Roses," done in 1883.

mine the elasticity modulus of wrought iron. Drawing on the early scientific studies of Robert Hooke, Thomas Young and others who had formulated elasticity principles for metals, Eiffel experimented until he had arrived at a workable formula good for all wrought-iron construction. His published memorandum on the subject took much of the guesswork out of calculating the effects of stress and strain on components of a given iron structure. It constituted an important addition to the small body of scientifically based quantitative calculation available to engineers of the day, many of whom were still relying on theories of structural analysis stemming from the sixteenth- and seventeenth-century studies of Palladio and Galileo. In Eiffel's own career, his formula became one of his most valued tools in creating the sturdy but light structures that became his hallmark, enabling him to reduce trusswork without sacrificing strength and rigidity. The resultant open webbing of his high bridge piers made them invulnerable to the nemesis of hundreds of bridges of the time: wind. Eiffel thus became a precursor of what Lewis Mumford later called "the architecture of the future, light, aerial, open to sunlight, an architecture of voids rather than solids."

Other innovations followed, as Eiffel's company was increasingly invited to bid for the big jobs. Most contracts were for the construction of railway bridges, for, although his company handled all forms of metal framework construction from factories to exhibition halls, train stations to churches, the sudden expansion of railways had ushered in the golden age of bridge building. Longer and higher bridges have been built since the latter half of the nineteenth century, but it is doubtful that as many have been constructed in a comparable period of time, or that their creators had to grapple with as many unknowns.

Writing their textbooks as they went, engineers independently evolved such tools as submersible pneumatic caissons for laying foundations on the bedrock of river bottoms, steel cable for sus-

40

pension bridges and a multiplicity of truss forms. Landmarks of this period included James B. Eads's immense bridge across the Mississippi at Saint Louis, completed in 1874, and the Brooklyn Bridge, built by John and Washington Roebling, that had a record 1600-foot central span suspended 120 feet above the East River and was finished in 1884. The greatest bridge of the century was the tremendous cantilever construction across Scotland's Firth of Forth, opened in 1890. Designed by Sir John Fowler and Benjamin Baker, the Forth railway bridge had two main spans of 1700 feet each, supported by steel trusswork 330 feet deep.*

Inevitably, the new technology took its toll as engineers groped to perfect their techniques. Besides fatal falls from high piers and other accidents, workers died of caisson disease, or the bends, while sinking foundations in compressed air chambers. Nor did all deaths occur during construction. With the weight of trains constantly increasing and bridge spans steadily lengthening, railway disasters occurred with alarming frequency — in the United States alone, 251 railway bridges failed in a ten-year period. Most sensational of the age's accidents was the Tay Bridge disaster in Scotland in 1878. Completed only a year before by Sir Thomas Bouch, the new wrought-iron bridge over the Firth of Tay was one of the largest and best known of the time. Sir Thomas had badly calculated his wind load factors, however, and a gale was blowing over the firth one December evening as an eight-car train carrying seventy-five passengers began to cross. Suddenly thirteen of the bridge's eighty-five spans gave way completely. The train and all its passengers were lost.

Not the least of Gustave Eiffel's achievements is that none of his bridges or other structures collapsed and most are still in use. Such durability was the result of the sort of creative attention to detail he showed in handling one of his first important contracts as head of his own firm, a bridge across the Sioule River north of

* By comparison, today's longest suspension bridge, the Verrazano-Narrows Bridge from Staten Island to Brooklyn, has a central span of 4260 feet.

Clermont-Ferrand, in France's tortuous Massif Central. Completed in 1869, the structure's 820-foot deck stood 262 feet above the river, making it one of the highest bridges in the world at the time and a direct ancestor of the Eiffel Tower. The Sioule bridge incorporated three innovations for Eiffel. First, while retaining cast iron for the vertical edges of his hollow, four-sided piers, he abandoned the heavy, brittle metal for the first time in favor of wrought iron — lighter and more elastic under wind loads — for the trusswork. Then he incurved the edges of the piers to give them increased footing and greater stability at the base. Finally, he developed a new method of "launching" the bridge's deck, utilizing a system of rollers on rockers, which supported the deck evenly as it was pushed straight out over the chasm to meet the next pier. All three of these Eiffelian traits — preference for wrought iron, careful attention to wind bracing and novel method of erection — are to be found in evolved form in the thousand-foot tower.

In the following years, Eiffel and Company constructed forty-two railway bridges and viaducts for French lines and began to bid in international competition for projects abroad. The Portuguese national railways chose him in 1875 for the delicate task of putting a bridge across the Douro river at Oporto. The great depth of the river at Oporto prohibited the use of a central pier, meaning that its 525-foot width would have to be spanned by other means. In the United States, the solution would likely have been a suspension bridge similar to that which John Roebling put over the Niagara in 1855, but in Europe engineers were leery of suspension bridges. Too many had failed, sometimes simply because marching men or herds of cattle accidentally struck a resonant frequency that set the bridges oscillating. Eiffel therefore designed a trussed parabolic arch to support the central span, and set the arch's sides at oblique angles to each other to give it extra wind resistance. Launching the arch, the largest ever attempted until then, was another problem, since supporting

42

*Construction of the bridge at Oporto in 1875, with the two halves
of the arch closing 200 feet above the Douro River.*

The Oporto bridge after completion.

scaffolding could not be erected in the river. Eiffel's ingenious solution was to build the two halves of the arch out toward each other, supporting them from above with steel cables attached to piers established on the banks. As work progressed, more cables were added to the gradually lengthening sections until the two halves joined like giant metal mandibles 200 feet above the center of the Douro. Completed in 1876, the magnificent bridge was christened the Maria Pia, in honor of the queen of Portugal.

Eiffel's triumph over the Douro led a French railway company operating in the Massif Central to contemplate a bridge at the record height of 400 feet above the rushing Truyère River at Garabit. Such a bridge would save twelve miles of track on the run from Marvejols to Neussargues — provided it could be built. The company approached Eiffel with the idea in 1879. He responded with plans for a bridge similar to the one at Oporto, but on a far grander scale: a height of 400 feet, length of 1850 feet, with the deck supported by five trusswork metal piers and a great parabolic arch with a 541-foot chord. The whole bridge would require 3587 tons of wrought iron and would cost $627,400. It

Construction of the bridge at Garabit, 1883, with its arches 400 feet above the Truyère River.

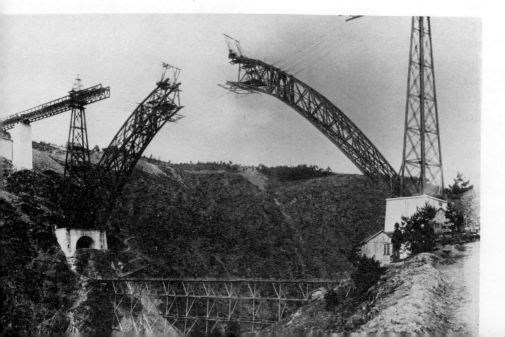

*When completed in 1884, the Garabit was the highest arched
bridge in the world.*

was to be the highest arched bridge in the world, the equivalent,
Gustave Eiffel liked to point out, of standing Paris' Vendôme
Column atop the spires of Notre Dame. Garabit would be ac-
claimed as "one of the victories of modern engineering"; it was
Eiffel's masterpiece until the construction of the thousand-foot
tower a decade later.

An undertaking of that size in France had to have the authorization of the Ministry of Bridges and Roads. After examining the
project the ministry gave its approval in June 1879, prudently
stating that Eiffel's successful completion of a similar bridge over
the Douro gave him a reasonable chance at Garabit, and acknowl-
edging that "M. Eiffel is the only person with such experience,
since it is he who invented the means of stiffening piers and
bridge deck against wind action." Eiffel went to work in his usual
methodical fashion, basing everything on meticulous computa-
tions. Stress in the trusses, for example, was to be limited to
exactly thirteen pounds per square millimeter under the combined action of train loads and wind, giving a cross-section of the

members 50 percent greater than if wind had been neglected as a load factor. He studied the effect of temperature changes on the metal components and found that pressure at the crown of the arch varied by only 1.39 pounds per square millimeter under a change of thirty degrees centigrade. Leaving nothing to chance, especially where wind was concerned, Eiffel figured in lateral pressure on the bridge deck with and without a train crossing it, taking into account exactly what percentage of the train's surface would be sheltered from wind by the deck's girders, and fixing in advance the velocity at which train traffic would be suspended. The Tay Bridge disaster would not be repeated at Garabit.

When the moment came to launch the tremendous arch, Eiffel proceeded much as he had at Oporto. Once the iron piers on either side of the Truyère had been raised, steel cables were fastened to them and dropped to the halves of the arch being built out from the bases of the piers. As more girders were riveted into place and the halves lengthened, additional cables were attached to the outer extremities, hanging them securely above the gorge. The breaking point of each cable was eighty-five tons, whereas during erection no cable actually bore more than fifteen tons. The job took slightly less than five years. When the proof load, consisting of a seventy-five-ton locomotive pulling twenty-two cars each weighing fifteen tons, moved ponderously across the Garabit Viaduct in November 1884, it was discovered that the loaded arch had a deflection of eight millimeters — precisely what Eiffel had predicted.

By the 1880s, the would-be vinegar maker from Dijon had become one of the world's master builders, working in the very

Tan An Bridge, Indochina, completed in 1880.

forefront of the technology of the age. The number and diversity of constructions undertaken by his company from 1867 to 1885 is astounding by any measure. They included:

• The Viana Bridge, Portugal. A combined road and railway bridge completed in 1877, the 2414-foot Viana was built on nine masonry piers sunk by Eiffel's compressed air method. The deck, weighing 1764 tons, was built entirely onshore and launched in one piece. It was the largest bridge deck ever to be so launched.

• The Pest train station, Hungary. A vast, ornate structure enclosing 140,000 square feet, the Pest station was completed in 1877. It was one of the first examples of the combined metal and masonry architecture that would become Art Nouveau, the principal decoration being the exposed metal components.

• The Tan An Bridge, Cochin China. One of many bridges built by Eiffel in French Indochina, the Tan An, completed in 1880, involved launching a clear span 262 feet across a deep, swift-running river, which made it impossible to establish supporting scaffolding. Eiffel divided the deck into two sections and pushed them toward each other in overhang until they met above the river and were joined. He utilized for the first time this "bootstrap" method that would enable him to put bridges across rivers and gorges that would otherwise not have been possible to span.

• Dome of the Nice Observatory. Eiffel built the iron trusswork and exterior of Charles Garnier's seventy-four-foot-diameter observatory dome, the largest of its day (1885). He added an original feature in establishing the rotating dome not on conventional rollers but on a frictionless floating ring that permitted easy turning of the 110-ton dome by hand.

The 110-ton dome of the Nice Observatory, completed in 1885, could be turned by hand.

Iron structural work at Bon Marché department store, Paris, 1879.

• Prefabricated campaign bridges. Designed for army use, these portable bridges were composed of a small number of standardized elements that could be assembled rapidly by non-specialized workers but were sturdy enough to support the passage of heavy artillery. Widely used by the French Army in Indochina, they were adopted by the Russian, Austro-Hungarian and Italian armies.

The list could go on, including gasworks, covered markets, iron framing for the church of Notre Dame des Champs in Paris, the Bon Marché department store and Musée Galliéra, buildings for the Paris Universal Exposition of 1878, and still more train stations and bridges in Europe, South America and Indochina. But the most important of Eiffel's structures yet unmentioned is universally known not for its usefulness but, like the thousand-foot tower, its symbolism. Perhaps appropriately, this thoroughly practical man was either to create or to be instrumental in building the best-known national symbols of the practical-minded modern world: the Eiffel Tower and the Statue of Liberty.

"Liberty Enlightening the World" was of course the work of Frédéric Auguste Bartholdi — except that once the Alsatian sculptor had designed his plaster model of the feminine figure with raised torch and spiked crown he was at a loss as to how to translate it into the colossus intended to symbolize Franco-American friendship. The figure was to be 151 feet tall, by far the greatest statue ever raised, with a head seventeen feet from chin to cranium, an index finger eight feet long and an extended right arm forty-two feet long and twelve feet thick. "Liberty" would dwarf the fabled statues of the ancient world, whether the sixty-six-foot-high Sphinx of Giza, the forty-foot Olympian Zeus, the 100-foot Colossus of Rhodes or the forty-foot Kamakura Buddha. But Bartholdi was uncertain what sort of construction would enable a statue of such size to be transported across the North Atlantic, set up on Bedloe Island and then bear its own weight and withstand the winds of the New York harbor. Masonry was out of the question. Bartholdi took the problem to Eiffel in 1881. The engineer whose career had been spent finding ways to subtract superfluous mass from enormous structures — proving that less is more somewhat before Mies van der Rohe got credit for the idea — designed an iron skeleton for a hollow statue. The surface would be sheets of metal attached to the interior framework. Bartholdi first tried bronze for the exterior but switched to copper sheets 3/32 of an inch thick when bronze proved too heavy. Eiffel designed a skeleton resting on vertical steel beams to be planted in the statue's granite pedestal. The most difficult technical problem was posed by the torch-bearing arm, which is in an inherently weak overhang position. Eiffel solved that by running the arm's supporting beams on through the body and across to the extreme left side, counterbalancing the overhang. The frame weighed only 162,000 pounds, compared to nearly 200,000 pounds for the hammered copper sheets of the exterior.

The long, frustrating process that had begun in 1875 when a French politician, Edouard René Lefebvre de Laboulaye, had formed the Franco-American Union to sponsor the statue as a gift to the United States at the Philadelphia Centennial Exposition of 1876, was finally bearing visible fruit. Difficulty in raising the $400,000 from private citizens to finance the project had caused Bartholdi to fall far behind the initial delivery date of 1876 (though part of the statue, the upraised torch, was displayed at Philadelphia), but by spring of 1883 the skeleton was standing in the work yards of Gaget, Gauthier & Company near the Rue de Chazelles in Paris' 17th arrondissement. For over a year, bemused Parisians watched the statue take shape behind its wooden scaffolding as workmen hung the 300-odd copper sheets on Eiffel's framework. Frequently the site was chosen by impromptu speakers who praised the idea of liberty as it was being defined and practiced in America. The French government, which had remained aloof from the project during the fund-raising phase, began to see it as a gesture that would gain good will for

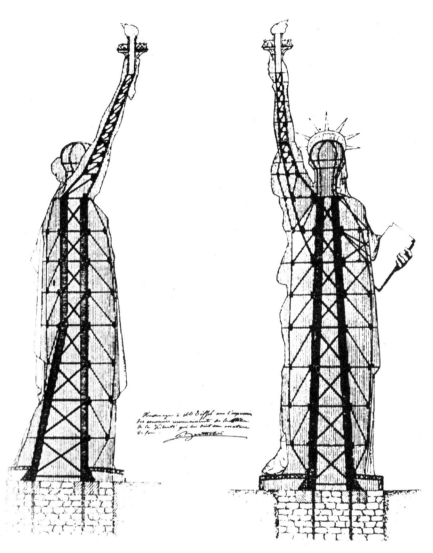

Interior bracing of the Statue of Liberty, 1881. Message signed Bartholdi reads "Praise to M. Eiffel with thanks from the Statue of Liberty who owes him her iron skeleton."

the Third Republic and incidentally combat the country's incipient monarchism by emphasizing democratic principles. It therefore offered the services of the French Navy in transporting the statue across the Atlantic. After Liberty was officially presented to the United States in a ceremony in Paris on July 4, 1884, the statue was dismantled, its metal components numbered and packed in eighty-five wooden cases and sent to Rouen. There the cases were loaded onto the three-masted French warship *Isère*, which arrived in New York in October 1885 to a cacophony of blaring tugboats and cheering if huddled masses.

Gustave Eiffel, an engineer living in the "glorious times" of his profession, was at the peak of his career. Contemporary photographs show him at fifty-five to have been small but well proportioned, with large, thickish hands, close-cropped, graying beard and hair, and heavy-lidded light blue eyes. If anything was remarkable about his generally unexceptional appearance it was his serene, hooded gaze, which gave him a look of complete self-possession free of interior conflict of any sort: dull company, perhaps, but one would feel safe crossing one of his bridges. Professionally, Eiffel had a self-confident mastery that led him to disdain secrecy; he routinely published the blueprints and calculations of his projects once they were completed. He was an engineer through and through, scorning superfluous embellishments, and was often heard to mutter "stupid as an architect" when exasperated by a bad design. In the rapidity and sureness with which he overcame technical problems, he appears to fit Paul Valéry's description of the great builders of the age, who "conceived their structures visibly as a complete whole rather than in two mental phases, one relating to form and the other to matter . . . they *thought* in materials." The one thing Eiffel lacked on the eve of the Paris Exposition of 1889 was fame, for he remained relatively unknown outside engineering circles. And it may be true, as Le Corbusier has suggested, that "He was pained by not being seen as a creator of beauty . . . His calculations were always inspired by an admirable instinct for proportion, his goal was elegance."

The thousand-foot tower he had proposed for the Exposition would make his name a household word in many lands and eventually even be considered beautiful by some. And whatever the great tower would come to mean to the generations who lived in its lanky shadow or who traveled far to see it, it gave a neat dramatic structure to the life of Gustave Eiffel. For the tower was not only his greatest metal construction, it was also his last.

FOUR

IT WOULD BE HARD to find a less martial terrain than the Champ de Mars. Bordered by some of the most prized real estate in Paris, it is a favorite park of chic *mamans* who wheel expensive English prams beneath its double rows of plane trees. Nearby, well-dressed children try for brass rings on the hand-cranked merry-go-round. There is not a uniform in sight, except for a bronze Marshal Joffre on horseback forever urging his troops to stand on the Marne, and the handful of park police quick to blow the whistle on toddlers or tourists who dare set foot on the manicured grass. The only armada is sailed in two small sparkling pools; the only shouts emanate from the excited young audience at a puppet show.

To be sure, the Champ de Mars has occasionally witnessed history. Louis XV founded the Royal Military School there and transformed the sandy plain into a parade ground where he could pass in review 10,000 men in battle formation arrayed from one end to the other. Hardy eighteenth-century French aviators found the area ideal for experiments, some successful, in their heated-air Montgolfiers. After the Revolution, secular holidays such as the Feast of the Federation were celebrated on the Champ de Mars, with Talleyrand saying Mass at a gigantic altar set in the middle of the field. When the Terror reigned, the unfortunate mayor of Paris, Bailly, was guillotined there. A triumphant Napoleon, a graduate of the Ecole Militaire ("Should make an excellent naval officer," a perceptive military mind noted on Bonaparte's application form when he entered), distributed the imperial standards to his victorious troops there in 1804. Thereafter, the area's military vocation declined, seemingly paralleling the fate of French arms. Horse races were its most important activity during the Second Empire, until the Longchamp track was created in 1855. During the great period of world's fairs, the Champ de Mars was the site of the Paris expositions of 1867, 1878 and of course 1889, as well as later ones in 1900 and 1937.

Beneath the surface, the Champ de Mars is much like the rest of Paris: gray plastic clay about fifty feet deep resting on a solid foundation of chalk. Its proximity to the Seine, however, has left it with an upper layer twenty feet thick of compact sand and gravel which slopes away toward the river. The closer to the Seine, the less stable the area's geological character, as Gustave Eiffel found when he received initial results of bore samplings of the tower site in early January 1887. In view of administrative complications, this threatened to be the first obstacle to his tower.

Except for a narrow band beside the Seine, which was the property of the City of Paris, the Champ de Mars belonged to the state. Negotiations with the government for a twenty-year lease of land for the tower would be long and drawn-out, and the one thing Eiffel did not have now was time. He could have immediate authorization from the city to build the tower on its land, but the samples raised questions about the stability of substrata there. Eiffel would have no problem with the tower's east and south feet, since they were far enough from the Seine to be on firm ground.*

* The base of the tower forms a square with 410-foot sides. The positions of its four feet correspond exactly to the cardinal points of the compass.

The north and west feet, however, would have to rest close beside the river, where the upper stratum was composed of soft alluvial deposits of sandy mud and clay mixed with such detritus as logs, pottery fragments, bones of domestic animals eons dead and masonry pieces from a long-buried wall. This would not do for foundations, and it remained to be seen at what depths the substrata became firm enough to support the tower. The soundings Eiffel had ordered from a subcontractor were inconclusive on this point, so he decided to conduct his own study. Using cylindrical pneumatic caissons seven feet in diameter, he dug to a depth of forty-eight feet. Workmen in the caissons turned up layers of sandy clay and fine sand above compact gravel which, if solidly based, could support foundations. To be certain, Eiffel bored five feet more and found what he was looking for: the good gray clay of Paris. If he sank the foundations for the Seine-side piers sixteen feet deeper than the other two, he would have solid

Pneumatic caissons used in sinking the tower's foundations, May 1887.

Cutaway view of the caissons in operation, with air lock at top and work chamber below.

footing for a thousand-foot tower weighing an estimated 10,600 tons, including heavy masonry bases under each foot.

Work began immediately on all four foundations. They did not have to go extremely deep, but since they were at or below the level of the Seine, excavation would be hampered by water seepage unless pneumatic caissons were used. Eiffel had had considerable experience with caissons in sinking his bridge foundations. On March 26, his shops began building sixteen iron caissons, four for each pier. Measuring fifty feet long, twenty feet wide and ten feet deep, each caisson had a work chamber six feet high within which several men could wield shovels and pickaxes. The men entered from the top through an air lock, and air pressure was kept high enough to repel below-surface water. The walls of the thirty-four-ton caissons were wedge-shaped at the bottom to form cutting edges, making the iron boxes sink as earth was hoisted out in buckets through airtight hatches. The interiors were illuminated by electricity, something of a luxury since electric lighting was just then being introduced in Paris homes.

Work proceeded rapidly — there were no cases of the bends, thanks to strict application of rules governing the rate of decompression when the men left the caissons — and when 40,500 cubic yards of earth had been removed from the four sites the foundations themselves were laid. Each pier would rest on a massive pile of cement and stone set obliquely in the earth so that the curving columns that bore the weight of the tower would exert their thrust at right angles to the mass. Into each excavation was poured a bed of quick-setting cement twenty feet deep to serve as a nonsettling base for the masonry. Over the cement, Eiffel placed enormous blocks of limestone quarried at Souppes-sur-Loing in central France, an area known for its solid travertine stone. The limestone in turn was capped by two layers of ultra-hard cut stone from Château Landon, the quarry that had provided the stone for the Arc de Triomphe and the Sacré Coeur basilica. Embedded in the center of each mass were two great anchor bolts twenty-six feet long and four inches in diameter, to

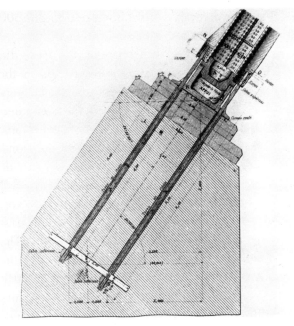

Diagram of foundation showing masonry, anchor bolts and cylindrical iron shoe with column attached. Piston can be seen in shoe, forming hydraulic jack for adjusting pier angle.

which a cylindrical flanged iron shoe was attached; the column would be bolted to the shoe and thus locked into the heart of the stone mass. Pressure from the columns was to be 10.2 pounds per square inch, whereas the stone could support 421 pounds per square inch — forty-one times the expected load. Additional excess safety was provided by the anchor bolts, which were not actually necessary to keep the tower from overturning, since theoretically it would be kept stable by its own weight.

Thus far, the tower's foundations were examples of classical civil engineering. The thoroughness and speed with which they were laid — they were in place on June 30, five months after the first spadeful of earth had been turned — were typical of Eiffel, but they involved no particular innovation. Where his innate inventiveness came into play, however, was in the design of the cylindrical shoes that would receive the columns. In the hollow of each shoe Eiffel placed a piston that could be moved by water under pressure. This was a truly brilliant stroke, for these hydraulic jacks gave him the ability to raise or lower each of the sixteen columns to insure that the piers were in a perfectly horizontal plane when the time came to join them with a band of girders at the first platform. If the piers, in their independent rise, were even infinitesimally out of plane, the deviation would throw the tower disastrously off vertical when it reached its full height. With the jacks, each capable of lifting 900 tons, Eiffel would be able to fine-tune the ungainly iron giant into perfect alignment.

Eiffel's calculations indicated that pressure on the earth beneath the masonry foundations would range from a minimum of fifty-eight pounds to a maximum of sixty-four pounds per square inch, depending on wind force and which pier was being considered. This was well within the limits that the substrata could bear. In fact, it is not much more pressure than a well-fed gentleman exerts on the floor when sitting on a spindly-legged chair.

The tower's relative lightness is one of the most astonishing things about it. As he had at the Douro and at Garabit, Eiffel reduced metalwork to the absolute minimum consistent with security; there was not an inch of superfluous trussing. To illustrate: if the tower's iron girders and braces were melted down and spread out into a square sheet equal in area to the four acres enclosed by its base, the sheet would be a mere two-and-a-half inches thick. And if an imaginary cylinder is conjured up with the tower's dimensions, that is, with a diameter equal to its base and a height of 1000 feet, the air in the cylinder would weigh nearly 10,000 tons, compared to the tower's 8000 tons of iron.

 Well before the first girder had been raised or rivet placed, Eiffel was certain of the tower's exact weight, and he could guarantee that the combined forces of gravity and wind, pulling and tearing year round at his lacy lattice, would not crumple it at some unpredictable moment of stress. True, he was working without such fundamental tools of modern engineering as electronic computers and systems engineering methods. Moreover, he was advancing into an uncharted area of technics. The "one exceptional way in which the project differed from works of earlier periods as well as from contemporary ones" has been described by Robert M. Vogel, curator of mechanical and civil engineering at the Smithsonian Institution in Washington. He observes that:

> In almost every case, these other works had evolved, in a natural and progressive way, from a fundamental concept firmly based upon precedent. This was true of such notable structures of the time as the Brooklyn Bridge and, to a lesser extent, the Forth Bridge. For the design of his tower, there was virtually no experience in structural history from which Eiffel could draw other than a series of high piers that his own firm had designed earlier for railway bridges.

And none of Eiffel's previous piers had reached even half as high as he now intended to go. Once again, Eiffel put his faith in figures and detailed planning. Soon after Maurice Koechlin and Emile Nouguier had presented their initial plan of the tower in 1884, he had his draftsmen turn out blueprints for every piece of metal to be used in it: 5329 mechanical drawings representing 18,038 separate items. These drawings alone took thirty draftsmen eighteen months to produce and covered 14,352 square feet of paper. Eiffel's greatest difficulty derived from the tower's odd angles. If it had been only an "assemblage of iron ladders," a few basic elements could have been designed and then copied thousands of times, as they had been for Eiffel's portable bridges. But the tower's curved, weight-bearing edges describe irregular

61

arcs and the trussing of its twenty-eight panels varies gradually from bottom to top. Each piece therefore had to be designed separately, taking into account the variable inclination of columns and braces along every foot of the tower's height. In addition, every rivet hole had to be drawn in at precisely the right spot, so that all the on-site workers would have to do was to place one-third of the 2.5 million rivets, the rest being placed at the shops in advance. The Eiffel Tower was one of the first examples of large-scale industrialized construction; all calculations had to be accurate to one-tenth of a millimeter.

When it came to determining the strength of the tower, Eiffel ignored the weight of visitors, despite the fact that the structure was designed to accommodate a maximum of 10,416 persons at one time on its three platforms. Their total weight, he figured, at an average of 154 pounds per person, would be 800 tons, or less than 10 percent of the tower's total weight. "The violence of the wind that we estimated in determining the strength of the tower," Eiffel explained later, "was so great that it would make visiting impossible. Besides, the visitors' weight produces negligible stress compared to that created by the weight of the tower itself and high winds."

The real problem was the wind. Eiffel knew his old enemy well and had outsmarted it in every one of his tall bridge piers. In designing the tower, he adopted two extreme hypotheses to simulate wind force. In the first, Eiffel took into account a wind of 134 miles per hour exerted evenly over the tower's entire surface from top to bottom; in the second, a wind of 148 miles per hour at the top, diminishing gradually to 105 miles per hour at the bottom. Never had winds of such force been observed in Paris. In addition, the surface to be struck was deliberately exaggerated. The upper half of the structure was assumed to be a solid surface taking the wind full-face; the intermediate area, where the open spaces are much greater, was figured to be four times its actual surface; below that, the four piers were assumed

62

to be solid surfaces rather than open trusses. Then coefficients for vertical weight and wind force were combined to give a total working coefficient for the entire tower and each of its twenty-eight trusswork panels. The figures showed that the mathematical center of the wind's action in the first hypothesis would be at a height of 278 feet, and in the second, 323 feet. The wind's total force, or overturning moment, was then compared with the tower's predetermined resistance to overturning, or moment of stability, considering its weight, height and base area. The moment of stability was greater. The tower would stand because of Eiffel's grasp of a paradox: victory over wind is achieved not through an accumulation of brute force, but by reducing the supporting elements of an openwork structure until the wind has virtually nothing to seize. Otherwise stated, the real strength of the Eiffel Tower is in its voids as much as in its iron.

On July 1, the tower began to rise. The jagged stumps of its four colossal box piers, inclined toward the center of the base area at an angle of fifty-four degrees, seemed to reach a little

Foundations of the south pier were ready in April 1887, with anchor bolts in place.

farther toward each other every day. Finished iron pieces arrived regularly by horse-drawn drays from Eiffel's shops in Levallois-Perret, about three miles away. During construction his shops would turn out up to 400 tons of girders and trusses per month. The pieces were hoisted into position by tall, steam-powered cranes. Eiffel deliberately used girders weighing no more than three tons, a relatively light maximum weight in view of the size of the structure. He had learned that using small components was faster and safer, even if this method did require more riveting, for cranes could be smaller and more mobile. The chances of accidents were reduced, and if one did occur the consequences were less serious. Use of bigger girders would have slowed the entire operation and required more expensive and complicated construction methods.

As it was, Eiffel's team of experienced workmen — most had been with him at Garabit, some even before — erected the lower piers with assembly-line speed. First they placed temporary pins in joints, then replaced these with bolts and finally rivets as

Jean Compagnon, Eiffel's foreman during construction of the tower.

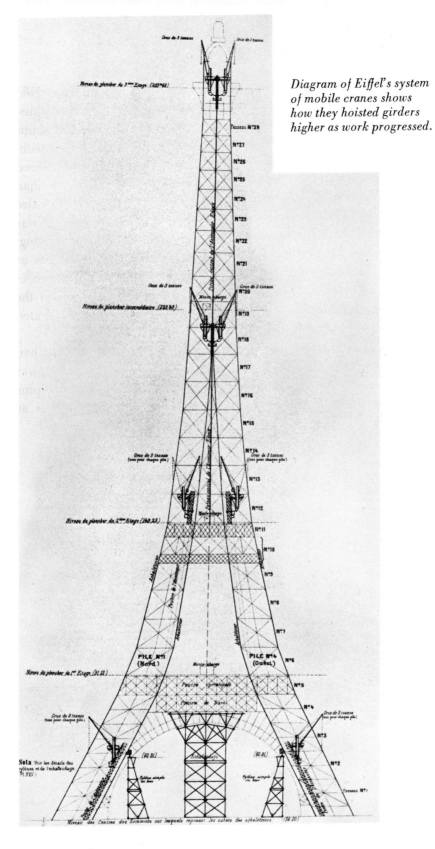

Diagram of Eiffel's system of mobile cranes shows how they hoisted girders higher as work progressed.

related pieces moved into position. The crew was small for such a project, never numbering more than 250 on the site. It was supervised by one of Eiffel's most trusted veterans, Jean Compagnon. Fifty years old, Compagnon had begun working on metal railway bridges in 1859 as foreman for the French construction company that built the bridges for the line from Saint Petersburg to Warsaw. He joined Eiffel and Company in 1876, and subsequently was foreman on all the company's important jobs, including the Maria Pia and Garabit.

When the columns began to approach the tops of the cranes, Eiffel shifted to an ingenious system of creeper cranes inside the piers themselves. Mounted on the inclined tracks that would later be used by the tower's elevators, the thirteen-ton cranes could pivot 360 degrees and be moved up the tracks periodically to

A pier begins to rise, July 1887.

follow the construction as it progressed. They were the heart of Eiffel's system at this stage and greatly impressed visitors to the site, such as the newspaper reporter who came away to write: "It is curious and interesting to watch these four lifting machines climbing ever higher along with the iron columns. They turn left, right, in, out, picking up the huge metal beams and placing them exactly where they are supposed to go."

As the columns rose, the moment drew nearer when their inclination would topple them unless they were given support. Eiffel's calculations predicted that this would happen — in technical terms, their centers of gravity would be located outside the area on which their bases rested — at a height of ninety-two feet. The columns were not to be joined until they reached the level of the first platform at 180 feet, so temporary bracing was neces-

Diagram of 90-foot wooden pylons that supported rising piers. Sand-filled metal cylinders for final adjustment of pier can be seen atop each pylon.

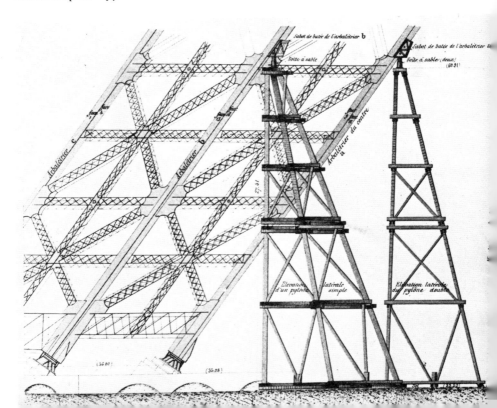

sary. Twelve wooden, derricklike pylons ninety feet tall were built and placed beneath the three interior columns of each pier. These were the first of two major scaffoldings required during the tower's construction. The other, begun shortly after the twelve pylons were in place, was composed of four platforms, each 150 feet high and eighty-two feet long, one in the center of every face of the tower. They were joined to form a square frame that would bear the increasing inward pressure of the piers as they rose above the ninety-foot pylons; the frame also supported the heavy iron girders and trusswork when they were raised to unite the piers permanently. The twelve pylons would have been no more than ordinary falsework had not Eiffel incorporated on their top platforms an adroit complement to the hydraulic jacks at the bases of the columns. This second system to be used in adjusting the angle of the piers was simplicity itself: sand-filled metal cylinders resting on the platforms and attached to the columns, accompanied by another set of hydraulic jacks. The cylinders were fitted with pistons at the top and plugs at the bottom. The columns leaned against the pistons. If a column was found to be too high by even a fraction of an inch, the plug could be pulled and the fine sand allowed to run out until the piston — and the column — was lowered to the correct position. If, on the other hand, a column was too low, the jack beside the cylinder could be operated to push the column back to the proper angle. If simplicity of conception and economy of means are signs of genius, it is such touches as these that define Eiffel.

The truncated piers reached ninety-two feet on October 10 and began leaning, imperceptibly, against the wooden pylons. Ten tons of iron had been mounted with 98,000 rivets. Somewhat before then it had become apparent even to the most skeptical Parisian that the mad structure might really be built, or at least that the attempt would continue until it ended in disaster. The latter eventuality was very much in the minds of some, particularly a number of solid citizens who lived near the Champ de Mars. It took little imagination to envision the gangling metal monster toppling onto nearby residences, and one nervous gentle-man was sufficiently shaken by the prospect to bring suit against the City of Paris to stop construction. Work came to a halt. Time, whose wingèd chariot had harried Eiffel ever since the Exposition committee had dawdled for months over its decision, threatened to overrun him unless the suit could be resolved rapidly. The city fathers had confidence in Eiffel — up to a point. They refused to accept responsibility for damage to persons or property caused by the thousand-foot tower. The buck stopped at Eiffel, who, having already done most of the financing of the project, now agreed to undertake construction at his own risk and to be en-tirely responsible for any accidents. If the tower proved danger-ous, he would be charged with its demolition.

Following the artists' protest, this second brouhaha over the tower was the last concerted effort to stop its construction, but it would be a long time before all doubt and concern were laid to rest. One French mathematics professor predicted flatly that if the structure ever reached the height of 748 feet, it would in-eluctably collapse. As the tower's shadow lengthened, many people peered intently at it on sunny days, watching for signs of wavering. Lightning and electricity were little understood by the popular mind, and some feared that burying conduits from the tower's lightning rods in the bed of the Seine would kill the fish. James Gordon Bennett's Paris edition of the New York *Herald* found the tower an easy target, sneering at "the modern Tower of Babel" and reporting that it had changed electrical conditions of the city. "The frequency of heavy storms which do not clear the air is taken by many to bear out this theory," the paper ex-plained. "People who have watched the tower closely and atten-tively have remarked the large quantities of heavy rain and thunder-clouds which gather round it and then, as if deprived by the lightning conductors of part of their electricity, are blown farther on and break in showers far away in quite another part of town." A popular Paris daily, *Le Matin*, headlined in early 1888, "The Tower Is Sinking." "If it has really begun to sink," the paper editorialized, "any further building should stop and sections already built should be demolished as quickly as possible."

Exactly the opposite was true, of course. The tower was rising so fast that Parisians could hardly believe their eyes. One of the most remarkable things about the tower's growth seems to have been how unobtrusively it was happening. It was compared to the steady, organic growth of a tree, imperceptible during a brief visit but constant and persistent. Due to Eiffel's meticulous planning of details, the prefabrication of most pieces and the small work force, there was little of the clamor usually associated with huge construction projects. A newspaper reporter visited the tower during these early months of its construction and gave this impression of the site:

I was standing at a height of about 200 feet, among a maze of ironwork painted with red lead, drilled with holes and arranged in crisscross fashion as far as the eye could see. Above a confused grayish mass of timber, and looking very small in such a grandiose setting, 250 workmen came and went in a perfectly orderly way, carrying long beams on their shoulders, climbing up and down through the latticed ironwork with surprising agility. The rapid hammer blows of the riveters could be heard, and they worked with fire that burned with the clear trembling flame of will-o'-the-wisps. The four cranes — one for each pillar — which brought up the pieces for this vast metallic framework one by one, stood out against the sky with their great arms at the four corners of this lofty site. During short winter days, when night falls the twenty rivet forges blaze in the high wind, casting a sinister glow over this tangle of girders until it acquires a fantastic aspect. The men work as late as possible and move about like shadows between these dark red smoky fires.

The smoothness of Eiffel's construction techniques contrasted sharply with the other great engineering project of the day, the

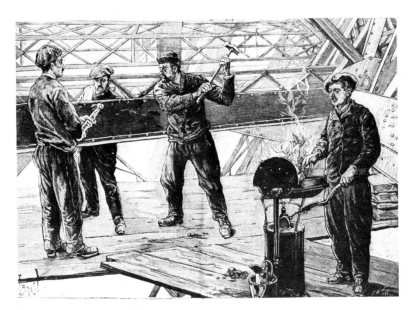

Riveting from a portable forge.

Forth Bridge in Scotland, then going up. As was the case on most British and American civil engineering projects, workers at the site received the elements of the colossal cantilever bridge in a semifinished state. They then had to consult blueprints and put the finishing touches to metal beams and trusses, shaping and drilling them to specification on the spot. The two projects were quite different, but it is safe to say that the thousand-foot tower would never have been ready for the Exposition of 1889 if not for Eiffel's prefabrication techniques. His twenty riveting teams had only to line up the tower's pre-punched holes and drive their glowing rivets home — in all, an average of 1650 rivets per working day during the period of construction. Eiffel was well on his way to setting, as one architectural historian later observed, "new world standards in the design and erection of very tall structures."

The quadrangular piers were now nearing the height of 180

Workers descending from their riveting platform.

feet and one of the most critical moments of the tower's rise. At this level, they would be joined together by an iron belt of horizontal trussing running from pier to pier. Twenty-five feet deep, the trussing would form the top of a pedestal with the piers as legs. On this the rest of the tower — another 800 feet of it — would sit. The trussing thus had to be rigid enough to unite the leaning piers into a solid base and also be perfectly horizontal. The question was whether the sixteen columns of the four piers would meet the belt at precisely the right height and at exactly the predetermined spots where the rivet holes had been bored. During their rise, the positions of the piers had been checked frequently by Eiffel's engineers with measured lengths of steel wire. Still, it was the first time Eiffel or any other engineer had attempted to maneuver iron piers weighing 440 tons, with dimensions roughly equal to the twin towers of Notre Dame Cathedral, within tolerances of only a few inches. When the piers were completed in early December, the girders of the trusswork were raised to the top of the four 150-foot platforms and riveted together. Then began the painstaking, infinitely delicate process of joining this massive iron frame to the piers.

This was the moment Eiffel had foreseen when he installed hydraulic jacks in the base shoe of each column and had positioned sand-filled cylinders atop the ninety-foot pylons. Moreover, during erection of the piers he had deliberately kept the columns slightly closer to the vertical than their final angle would be, so that ultimate corrections could be made by lowering rather than by raising the heavy beams. As if he were adjusting a gigantic precision instrument, Eiffel slowly brought the sixteen columns into line, slightly nudging one with a jack, minutely lowering another by releasing a small quantity of sand from a cylinder. When each column reached the proper height and angle, workmen drove iron wedges beneath it to fix it in place. So well thought out was the system that three or four men could align each tremendous pier; so well had the foundations been laid

The tower rises: January 7, 1888

April 27

June 12

July 19

September 19

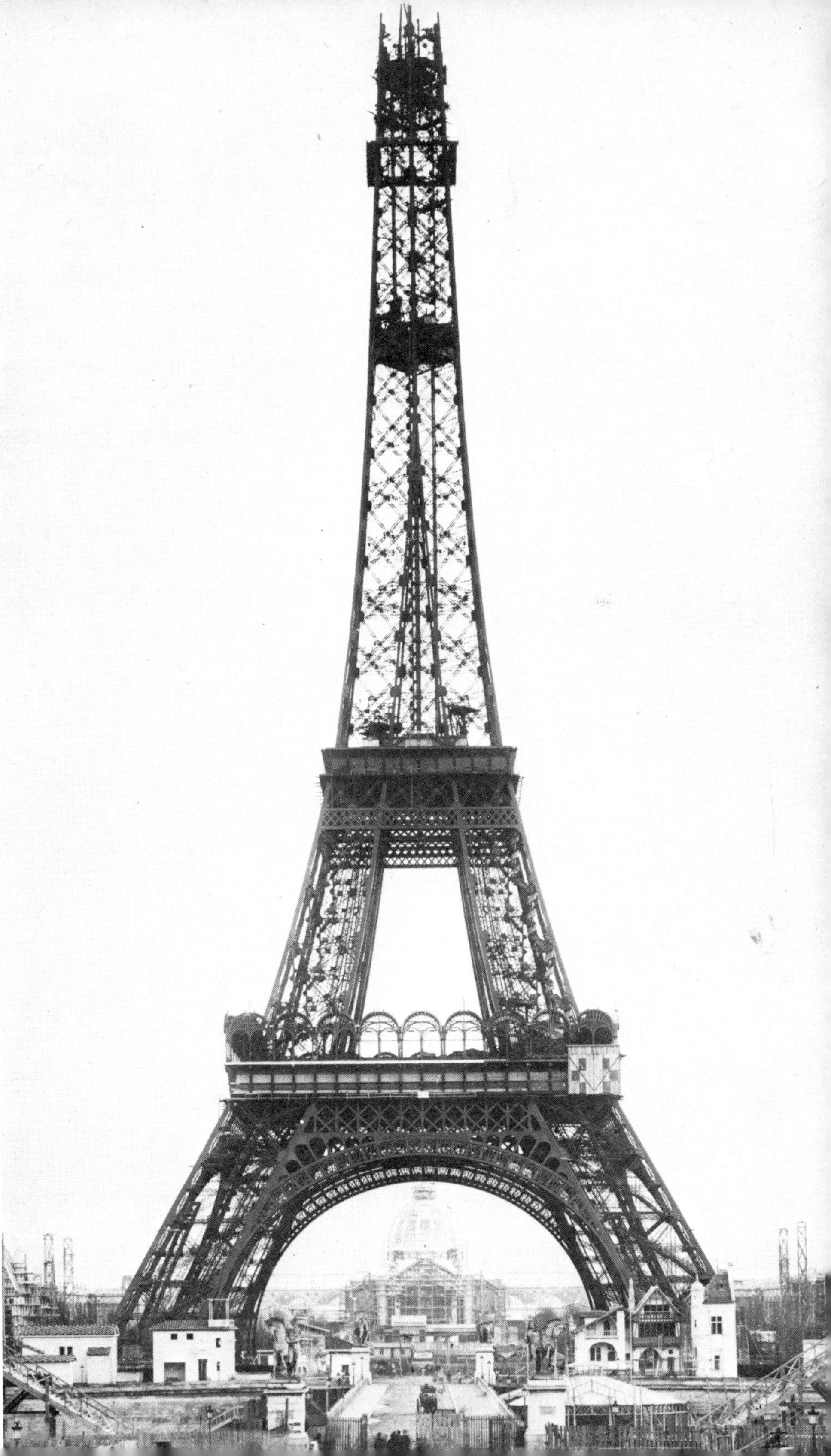

February 2, 1889

and the piers mounted that in no instance did more than two and one-half inches separate the outreaching beams from the horizontal frame.

On March 26, 1888, the operation was completed, without so much as a file or hand-drill being used to correct the alignment of the rivet holes. With barely more than one year remaining before the structure was due to open to the throngs expected at the 1889 world's fair, many Parisians thought the tower looked more like a hulking metal beast crouched on all fours than the immensely tall, graceful tower Eiffel had promised. But he knew that the essential had been accomplished. As he wrote later, "Joined by the belt of girders, the piers formed a solid table with a wide base. The sight of it alone was enough to brush aside any fear of its overturning. We no longer had to worry about a major accident, and any minor ones that might occur now could not compromise completion of the structure."

Eiffel's confidence at this point, in the success of his tower and in himself, was total. It may then have been an understandable excess of pride that led him to assume responsibility for still another project, even as the tower reached only the halfway mark. Vaster and still more daring than the tower, this task similarly promised to realize an old dream through methodical application of new technology.

A canal through the isthmus of Central America had fired imaginations since the day in 1513 when Balboa discovered that only about fifty miles of land separated the Atlantic from the Pacific in this part of the New World. In 1525, Hernando Cortez drew up a plan for joining the two oceans, and thereafter many maritime nations probed that narrow but intractable neck of jungle, swamp, mountain and river. Explorers repeatedly searched for the passage that would save up to 2000 miles on the voyage from Europe to the Pacific and cut nearly 8000 miles from the Cape Horn route from the East to the West coasts of the United

76

Fine-tuning one of the tower's sixteen columns, March 1888.
Workers at left operated pump to force water into hollow
shoe at base of column. When adjustment was completed, worker
at right drove iron wedges into place.

States. France and Holland, Britain and the United States surveyed the area, signed treaties with Colombia and Nicaragua, which controlled the isthmus, and fought diplomatic duels with each other over it. The first transportation link between Atlantic and Pacific came in 1855, when the United States completed a railway across Panama.

Projects for the canal became a standard subject at international geographical conferences in Europe, such as the ones in Antwerp in 1871 and in Paris in 1879. The latter meeting, the International Interoceanic Canal Study Conference, was presented with some fifty plans for canals — across Nicaragua, across Panama, with locks, at sea level. The meeting was dominated by the impressive, white-maned figure of Ferdinand de Lesseps, whose Suez Canal had opened in 1869. Now a vigorous seventy-five — ten years previously he had married an

77

eighteen-year-old Creole girl by whom he sired nine children — Lesseps had been dubbed a *Grand Français* by his countrymen as a result of his having built the Suez Canal and enjoyed immense prestige in academic, financial and political circles. A diplomat by profession rather than a technician, he appears to have seen a Panama canal as the climax of his career, despite efforts by his son Charles to dissuade him. Moreover, he insisted at the Paris conference that a sea-level canal, without locks, would work in Panama just as it had at Suez. After two weeks of debate, the 135 engineers, businessmen, geographers and entrepreneurs attending the conference voted on May 29 in favor of the sea-level plan. Only eight conferees opposed the idea, maintaining that a system of locks would be necessary to negotiate such natural obstacles as the 400-foot-high Culebra range and the torrential Chagres River. One of the principal figures of this minority was Gustave Eiffel.

Lesseps was named president of the Panama Interoceanic Canal Company and began raising capital. He traveled as far as New York to promote the venture, stopping off to look over the Brooklyn Bridge then being built and speaking before the American Society of Civil Engineers. In France, the company's experts evaluated the costs of excavation and construction at $214 million, but Lesseps started out with the barely $6 million that came in mainly from small French investors impressed by his name and favorable articles in the press. Work began in 1882, and it rapidly became clear that Lesseps had seriously underestimated the difficulties of building the canal. Lesseps' general contractor, a Belgian firm, opted out after less than a year in the face of malaria and yellow fever epidemics that scythed through the ranks of workers, and the rocky Culebra that became unstable after every tropical rain and slid back into excavations as fast as they were made. By 1885, the Culebra had hardly been dented and costs were skyrocketing. Lesseps requested government authorization for a bond issue with a special lottery provision to spur public response, but was refused.

Desperate, Lesseps approached Eiffel in November 1887 and asked him to take over construction of the Panama Canal. Not only had Eiffel's perception of the task been accurate from the start, also he subsequently patented a system of metal locks capable of handling differences of water level as great as seventy feet at a time. Thus despite the animosity between the two men as a result of Eiffel's vote against Lesseps' sea-level plan, Eiffel plainly was the only hope left for the canal. Besides, Lesseps badly needed more capital and thought that a new sale of bonds to the public would succeed if the great engineer's name were associated with the project. Eiffel hesitated three weeks, then signed a $27.4 million contract with the Universal Interoceanic Panama Canal Company, as it had been renamed, to oversee all aspects of construction of the canal and to design, fabricate and install ten locks. Considering that Lesseps had been floundering in the swamps of Panama for six years and the work was still barely begun, the deadline Eiffel accepted for completion and opening of the canal was, to say the least, astonishing: July 1, 1890 — thirty months to push a canal through the treacherous isthmus, including a system of locks that had never been tried on such a scale, the job to be financed by a company that had been plagued with money problems since its founding. For once, Eiffel's prudent Burgundian judgment appears to have been clouded.

In any case, he was committed to the work and began executing it in January 1888 with his customary thoroughness and speed. The giant locks, sliding metal gates seventy-nine feet wide, sixty-nine feet high and thirteen feet thick, were subcontracted to a firm in Nantes. Altogether they would enable a ship to be raised or lowered 330 feet, the maximum difference between the Atlantic and the Pacific. By February he had 2500 workers on the Panama site; by August over 6000. As of August 25, 1888, barely eight months after taking over the job, Eiffel had excavated 630,000 cubic yards of earth and was in that respect nearly ten months ahead of the schedule called for in his contract. He had on order 30,000 tons of cast iron for his locks, as well as 28,000 tons of cement and 26,000 tons of crushed stone for the masonry parts. Never had prospects appeared so favorable. In June the government had authorized Lesseps to float the bond issue refused three years earlier, bringing the company $51 million in new capital. For the first time since the project got under way eight years earlier, it began to look very much as if the Panama Canal, coveted for centuries by many nations, would after all be French.

In Paris, the completion of the first platform in March 1888 gave Eiffel his launching place for the rest of the tower. The first thing he did to prepare for the final phase of the ascent to one thousand feet was to set up a steam-powered crane on the platform to hoist materials from the ground. Tracks were laid around the platform's circumference and wagons like miniature boxcars were used to carry materials from the central crane to the four creeper cranes. Workers were putting in twelve-hour days during the spring and summer, and in order to obviate their having to descend to the ground for lunch, losing more time each day as the tower rose, Eiffel installed a canteen on the platform. This had the additional advantages of preventing excess fatigue — workers had to climb temporary stairs and ladders to reach their jobs, there still being no elevators — and giving Eiffel a measure of control over on-the-job drinking, a common problem on French work sites. Sale of cognac and other strong drink was forbidden in the canteen, but this absence was compensated for by substantial meals, including a ration of wine, for which the workers paid only a nominal price, Eiffel subsidizing the real cost. When the second platform was completed at a height of 380 feet, the canteen was moved up to it.

The second level was attained in early July 1888, and on the fourteenth, Bastille Day, a fireworks display was shot off from the new height to the pleasure of crowds gathered across the

Seine at the Trocadéro. That day, Eiffel held a banquet on the first platform for members of the Paris press. He took the occasion to deliver a pep talk. "Judging by the interest that the tower seems to inspire both in France and abroad," he declared, champagne glass in hand, "I believe it is fair to say that we are showing the world that France continues to be the leader of progress and that she is realizing a project which has often been tried or dreamed of. Only through the advancement of science, metallurgy and the art of engineering that distinguish the latter part of our century have we been able to surpass the generations which preceded us. Construction of this tower will be one of the landmarks of modern industry that made it possible." The sentiment was pure Victorian, the rhetoric probably a mixture of conviction and press-agentry. Even so, Eiffel, an imaginative engineer but never one to strain for original phrasing when a platitude would do, once again showed a canny understanding of what the tower meant to his country, and what it would eventually mean to a technophilic world.

FIVE

As THE TOWER ROSE, so did pay for its builders. During the first twelve months of construction, pay rates ran from eight cents an hour for unskilled laborers to fourteen cents an hour for qualified metalworkers. In July 1888 wages for both categories rose by one cent, followed by another one-cent raise in September. In addition, Eiffel now assumed payment of accident insurance, which until the first platform was reached he had paid by withholding 2 percent of workers' pay. But as the tower neared two-thirds of its ultimate height, the workers' unrest grew, reinforced by an awareness that the Paris Exposition could not very well open with its vaunted tower half-finished. Admittedly, work had often been arduous and not without danger and discomfort. Vertigo seems not to have troubled the workers; wooden platforms had been built out around their positions to help them avoid seeing straight down. Still, a fall was always possible. Besides the danger of death, there were the usual hazards of outdoor construction work, often magnified by the tower's height and its deliberately open design that afforded slight shelter from wind. During the winters of 1888 and 1889, workers perched on girders hundreds of feet above the Seine suffered bitterly from

Wooden platforms built out around columns helped prevent vertigo.

icy winds that froze fingers to metal and cooled rivets before they could be driven.

When construction of the Eiffel Tower began, French labor was just beginning to become conscious of its potential power. Whereas there were on the average only forty strikes per year in France between 1874 and 1880, the figure rose to 175 for each year from 1886 to 1889. Labor unions had been legalized in the country in 1884. The tower was a vulnerable target for a strike, and soon after the first platform was finished worker representatives began demanding higher hourly rates. On September 19, with working days growing shorter and pay packets shrinking as a result, workers on the tower laid down their tools, bringing the whole, finely coordinated operation to a halt. They demanded a flat raise of four cents an hour for all categories of workers, ap-

plicable immediately. Eiffel countered with a proposal for a one-cent per hour raise for skilled workers only. After three days of bargaining, a progressive formula was worked out under which all workers would receive one cent per hour more each month, up to a maximum of four cents' increase.

Work was resumed on this basis until mid-December, when the tower stood at 645 feet. With raises under the September formula reaching their maximum and Paris temperatures heading for their annual minimum, work stopped once again. This time Eiffel refused to budge on salaries, although he promised a special bonus to all workers who stayed on the job until the tower was completed. Workers not present the following day would be fired. Most workers did show up the next day, and the few who did not were easily replaced. Strike leaders were taken off assembly jobs on the upper reaches of the tower, put to work building the first platform arcades and forbidden to go higher, a calculated slap at their professional pride. Sarcastically called *les indispensables* by the other workers, most eventually quit their jobs. Thereafter the tower was free of labor strife. When it was completed Eiffel had the names of 199 loyal workers, from Alézy to Zettelmaier, painted on a girder in full public view.

From the foundations to the second platform, the tower is composed of four quadrangular piers joined into a rigid whole by horizontal bands of girders beneath each platform. From the second platform to the top, however, the four distinct piers converge at a point slightly above the second platform into a single vertical column formed by their exterior faces. Thus there were no longer four creeper cranes to follow the tower's ascent, and Eiffel had to alter his method of rapidly getting the girders, rivets and other materials into position for assembly. His solution was to put new cranes on the vertical beams rising in the center of the tower that later would guide elevators to the third platform. Placed back to back, the cranes counterbalanced each other and

85

Left: *Work on the Exposition grounds as the tower reaches its second platform, July 1888.*

had enough reach to service all points of the converging sides of the tower. To give them sufficient support on the narrow column, auxiliary iron frames thirty feet high and twelve feet wide were bolted to it and the cranes attached to them. When the two cranes had traveled up the thirty-foot stretch of frame, another frame was placed atop the first and the cranes clambered on. The time required to make the shift from one frame to another was only thirty hours, a quick operation considering that the cranes and their frames weighed fifty tons. Eiffel now had four hoisting systems operating simultaneously: a steam winch on the first platform raising material from the ground, another on the second platform relaying it on to a third winch set on an intermediate platform at 650 feet, which passed materials and whole, prefabricated truss panels to the swiveling creeper cranes. A three-ton girder could be hoisted into position in only twenty minutes. This system was key to Eiffel's construction technique as he raced against the opening day deadline.

By now the tower was drawing an increasing number of curious visitors as eager for a view of Paris never before seen, except by a few balloonists, as for a look at the structure itself. One made the climb on a blustery winter day and duly recorded his impressions in the mauve prose affected by French newspapers, incidentally giving us some insight into Gustave Eiffel's climbing prowess:

Indian file, with M. Eiffel in the lead, we start up the staircase. At that moment the thermometer says 30 degrees. The weather is still threatening, but snow has stopped falling. M. Eiffel advises me to imitate his gait. He climbs slowly, with his right hand on the bannister. He swings his body from one hip to the other, using the momentum of the swing to negotiate each step. Here the incline is so gradual that we can chat as we climb, and no one is winded when we reach the first platform.

At this height the city already appears immobile. The silhouettes of passersby and fiacres are like little black spots of ink in

*Fifty-ton mobile cranes counterbalanced each other above
the second platform.*

*Eiffel with a group of Paris journalists after hosting a
lunch for them, July 1888.*

the streets. Only the rippling Seine seems still alive. To the south
there is a fine view of the Exposition grounds, with the glass roof
of the Machinery Hall looking like a lake of molten lead. I peek
through a crack in the wooden flooring and look straight down
into the void. Far below, I can see very small ducks swimming in
a half-frozen pond. A shiver runs down my spine at the thought of
a possible fall from this height.

Continuing up the staircase, the cold iron railing hurts my
fingers so much that I try to climb with my hands in my pockets,
but the wind buffets me and I am blinded by driving sleet. So I
grab the railing again and shield my face with my arm. All I can
see is M. Eiffel's coat ahead.

At the height of 900 feet there is a wind of only fifteen miles per
hour, but it is enough to take my breath away. Workers here are
placing a rivet. The great nail is taken red-hot from its portable
forge, positioned in the hole and struck with heavy hammers in a
shower of sparks. Below, Paris seems to be sinking into the night

like some fabled city descending to the bottom of the sea amid a murmur of men and church bells.

We return to the second platform for hot drinks in the canteen. M. Eiffel says that congratulations are coming in from all over, even from some of the artists who signed the famous protest. "There are only three or four stubborn writers still holding out," he says. "I really don't understand why." Conversation drags on lazily. We are reluctant to leave the warmth of our shelter to go back into the wind which seems to weep with the sound of human sobs in these hundreds of feet of iron stretched from earth to the clouds like an eolian harp.

As late as early 1889, visitors had to climb stairs and ladders to see the tower — and Paris from the tower — because its elevators were not yet functioning. In fact, the tower's passenger elevators were one of the stickiest technical problems that faced Eiffel. In this area he had to rely entirely on subcontractors, and appears to have felt considerable frustration at seeing this major element of the construction escape his control. The Exposition committee was particularly concerned about the elevators. While many visitors would likely be willing to climb the 363-step staircases in the east and west piers to the first platform, they could not be expected to go much farther on foot — it was another 381 steps to the second platform. (A narrow spiral staircase of 927 steps led from the second platform to the top, but was for use by the tower's personnel only.) Fast, comfortable elevators therefore were essential to the public's enjoyment of the tower, but the committee insisted first and foremost that Eiffel give every guarantee of their absolute safety. It was casting worried glances over his shoulder on every decision concerning the elevators, and reserved the right to veto any design that did not appear to meet its unconditional requirements.

Several factors compounded the problem of getting visitors to the top, with intermediate stops at the first and second platforms. The height to be scaled was far greater than any ever attempted, as were the numbers of passengers to be transported — thousands per day if the public were not to be discouraged by long waiting lines from making the ascent. Then too, the tower's curving piers, where the elevators were to be installed, required a design different from the usual straight vertical approach, or even a straight incline. From a ground-level angle of fifty-four degrees, the piers arched to seventy-eight degrees at the second platform. The elevators would have to travel either on tracks with a constant curvature or on tracks that approximated two straight runs at different angles. In neither case did the past experience of elevator makers in Europe or America provide a ready answer to the technical difficulty involved.

The state of the art was primitive. Steam-powered hoists, mainly for freight, had come into use in the 1860s, but the cumbersome drums they needed to take up supporting cables limited them to a rise of about 150 feet. Systems utilizing a screw and traveling nut were slow and suitable only for low-rise lifts. The most practical elevators of the day incorporated a cylinder and piston power source, with the piston moved by water pressure. Attached to the elevator's cables, which passed over a sheave at the top of the shaft, the piston had its action multiplied by pulleys to give the desired length of rise. This so-called hydraulic, rope-geared method had been developed into an effective elevator system by the 1880s, principally in America by the Otis Elevator Company. But in the view of European engineers, it had one major drawback: the cabin was suspended from above rather than pushed from below. Just as suspension bridges were generally avoided in Europe in favor of arched bridges, suspension elevators were considered less safe than the direct plunger type, which rested on a piston that rose and fell as a cylinder was filled with water or emptied. Linear descendant of an ordinary hydraulic press, the plunger elevator was proof against accident, but its rise was directly related to piston length. This was an awkward arrangement at best, and an impossible one in the case

90

of the tower's lower elevators since a 220-foot cylinder well would have had to be bored right through the masonry foundations.

When construction of the tower began, Eiffel appointed an engineer named Backmann to study the elevator problem. Backmann skipped the whole knotty question of getting to the second platform and concentrated on the long but straight run from there to the top. For that he proposed a suitably complicated system involving a nut and bolt arrangement that would, in effect, "screw up" the cabin on a helicoidal shaft. There would be two cabins on parallel shafts, traveling in opposite directions to counterbalance each other. The most novel touch was that each cabin would be powered independently by an electric motor, an idea that was ahead of its time since electric power was not successfully used in elevators until the turn of the century. The committee was not convinced, however, and, wary of the scheme's complexity, noise and electric power, rejected the proposal in mid-1888.

Eiffel contracted with two French firms for the relatively easier elevator jobs, that is, ground to first platform and second platform to top, both allowing a straight run. For the more difficult task of negotiating the curve to the second platform, however, no French elevator maker bid on the job. This left Eiffel in a pretty fix, for the Exposition's charter prohibited use of foreign equipment in constructing the tower, and the only candidate for the remaining contract bore the unfortunate name of American Elevator Company, the European branch of Otis, which submitted a bid through its Paris office, Otis Ascenseur Cie. The Exposition committee duly rejected the company's initial bid, but when an extended bidding time expired without a French proposal, the committee gave in and awarded a $22,500 contract to Otis. The tower's elevators would comprise three entirely different systems installed by three different companies. The efficiency of such an arrangement was questionable but proved workable. It is perhaps this difficulty in finding a smooth, rational way to transport visitors that most graphically illustrates how unprecedented the tower was as an engineering project. Viewed from a distance, the structure appears simple, like a force of nature, a graceful iron geyser shooting from the earth. But, as when one watches a magician's act from the wings, a closer look reveals the tower to be full of busy sleight of hand. Those magnificent circular arches between its legs, for example, that most visitors assume support the tower, actually bear no load at all. With their stylized floral motif, their role is purely decorative — and perhaps psychological, Eiffel knowing that the public would "understand" a structure supported by arches but feel less at ease with one resting only on curving pylons.

When the tower's elevator systems are contemplated, however, beads of perspiration become visible on the magician's brow. Consider the scrambled scenario for getting visitors up: to the first platform, elevators in the east and west piers; to the second, one elevator in the north pier that stops on the way at the first level and in the south pier another that runs only between the first and second platforms; above the second platform, a double elevator to the top, requiring a change of cars at an intermediate level. Compared to the spare, intelligent economy that marks most of Eiffel's work, the tower's system of internal transportation appears conceptually cumbersome. Technical problems aside, the design of the elevators was in good measure dictated by aesthetic reasons, for Eiffel refused to consider elevators that rose straight from the ground up through the center of the tower. Such a system would have spoiled the structure's uncluttered purity of line, distracting the eye with shafts, cables and cabins from the arches and their forceful visual impression of wide-straddled space. He was certainly right on that count. And in favor of the elevator systems finally adopted it must be said that despite their clanking, Heath Robinson complexity, they did do the job: the trip to the top of history's tallest manmade structure took only seven minutes, and 455 persons per hour could

92

make it. At the lower levels, 1800 visitors per hour could be hoisted to the first platform, 882 to the second.

Of the three systems, the Otis was the simplest in design: a hydraulic, rope-geared unit of the sort that had become standard since about 1880. Its thirty-six-foot-long cylinder was inclined at an angle parallel to the car's initial run. It incorporated a piston thirty-eight inches in diameter attached to cables running through a huge tackle composed of five fixed and six movable pulleys. As water from a reservoir on the second platform forced the piston through the cylinder, the cable-suspended, double-deck car was pulled along a set of rails that curved once at the first platform to accommodate the increasing angle of the tower's leg. The result was fast — 400 feet per minute — quiet, vertical transportation. Otis had worked on the design for three years, confident long before getting the contract that the Exposition committee would accept its bid.

Although the car was fitted with spring-loaded brake shoes that would automatically grab the rails if any of the six cables broke, a heated dispute developed between Eiffel and Otis over the elevator's safety. Probably pushed by the committee, Eiffel insisted that Otis use the rack and pinion safety system installed on many of Europe's cog railways. The American firm objected that cogs would be noisy and would unnecessarily restrict the elevator's speed. When Eiffel and an Otis representative sent over from New York failed to reach an accord, Otis simply threatened to withdraw from the project. Nothing further was said about the matter, and cogs were never installed. To dispel any public apprehension over the safety of this — for Europeans — unconventional suspension method, Eiffel conducted a dramatic test before putting the Otis elevators into service. On one of the elevators he replaced the steel cables with hemp ropes, then raised the car about fifteen feet and cut the ropes. The automatic brakes caught and the nineteen-ton car descended slowly to its base.

Before the tower was completed, Eiffel again crossed swords

The Otis elevator system.

with Otis — and again lost. The contract with Otis called for the elevators in the north and south piers to be in operation by January 1, 1889. Because of the number of modifications made during installation, Otis found this impossible, but guaranteed that the elevators would be functioning by May 1, the Exposition's opening day. Eiffel said he would refuse to pay for work that did not meet the contractual deadline. That prompted an enraged Charles Otis to set the trans-Atlantic cable sizzling with a telegram: "After all else we have borne and suffered and achieved in your behalf," Otis fumed, "we regard this as a trifle too much; and we do not hesitate to declare, in the strongest terms possible to the English language, that we will not put up with it." He threatened once more to quit — "and Mr. Eiffel must charge to himself the consequences of his own acts." The ultimatum left Eiffel outgunned, and with time running out he had no alternative

94

but to pay. He got his money's worth in the end, for although the Otis elevators were not both in operation until mid-June, they worked so well that they were considered one of the most effective American technical exhibits at the Exposition.

French elevator makers were represented on the tower by two companies: Roux, Combaluzier and Lepape for the elevators in the east and west piers to the first platform, and Edoux for the vertical run from the second platform to the top. Both systems were ingenious. True to their prejudice against suspension elevators, the French engineers at Roux opted for a technique based on the well-tried direct plunger method. Since a 220-foot cylinder well was impracticable under the circumstances, they found a way to push up the elevator car with what was in effect a flexible piston. Their solution was a chain of three-foot-long articulated links running through an iron conduit. Rollers in each link's joints were intended to reduce friction within the conduit but succeeded only marginally. Powered by hydraulic cylinders similar to those used by Otis, large sprockets at the tower's base fit like gears into the links to force them up or to let them descend at a regulated pace under the weight of the car. The system was extremely complicated, and the hundreds of links rolling against the interior of the conduits produced both excessive friction — five times as much as the Otis system — and noise. But such was the price the French were prepared to pay in the interest of absolute safety. In Eiffel's opinion, the system was "not only safe, but appeared safe, a most desirable feature in elevators traveling such heights and carrying the general public." Significantly, this method was never again used, an indication that while it worked well enough on the Eiffel Tower it was far too unwieldy to have a future. The Roux cars were double-decked and could carry one hundred passengers, compared to forty for the Otis cars, but were only about half as fast: 200 feet per minute, as opposed to nearly 400 feet per minute for the Otis.

With the Roux elevators carrying passengers to the first platform and the Otis system servicing the second platform directly from the ground via the north pier and shuttling between the first and second platforms via the south pier, Eiffel still had to get the most intrepid visitors to the top. He awarded the contract to Leon Edoux, a schoolmate at the Ecole Centrale and a leading French elevator manufacturer. Edoux's speciality was the plunger system, but the problem of installing a piston elevator with a rise of 526 feet was, like most of the tower's technical challenges, unprecedented. Not only was the length of rise over twice that of the highest piston elevator then in service, but aesthetics dictated that the plunger cylinder not infringe upon the open areas beneath the second and first platforms. If the conventional approach were taken and the piston placed at the bottom of the

The Roux-Combaluzier elevator with its system of articulated rods.

run — the second platform — its cylinder would extend below to a distance equal to the car's rise, projecting downward through the center of the tower and burying itself 146 feet deep in the middle of the base area. Such an eyesore was unthinkable.

Edoux's solution was a brilliant compromise between the piston and cable-suspended elevator systems. First, he divided the vertical run into two equal parts. Two cars would be used, one ascending the first 263 feet, the other going on to the top. Passengers changed cars at an intermediate level. This enabled Edoux to put slender twin pistons, which presented less surface to the wind than one large one, beneath the car running to the top, and since they needed to be only 263 feet long they would not project below the second platform. Water to fill the cylinders was in a reservoir on the top level. With the two runs parallel but on either side of the tower's central guide rail, the cars, connected by steel cables running over sheaves at the top, counterbalanced each other. Here was the compromise: the car running from the intermediate level to the top rested on the two pistons, but the one operating from the second platform was suspended. Thus the upper car was obviously safe resting on the pistons, but the lower one must have given the committee — and perhaps Eiffel — some uneasy nights because a break in the suspension was not altogether impossible. Nor was it likely, of course; the four steel cables used were rated at over two million pounds of breaking stress. The maximum load possible in the two cars under any condition being 47,000 pounds, that meant a safety factor of forty-three, enough to reassure even the most punctilious engineer. As an added safety measure, however, automatic brakes were installed in the lower car to grip the guide rails if the car's speed exceeded a set rate. At a vertical speed of 180 feet per minute, sixty-five passengers could make the trip in four minutes, including the transfer from the lower car to the upper, which took about one minute.

Water for all five hydraulic elevators was taken from the Seine

97

and recycled to the reservoirs on the second and third platforms by steam-powered pumps located in an underground machine room beneath the south pier. Interestingly, the pumps for the Otis and Roux elevators were French, as might be expected, but the ones for the Edoux system were American-made Worthingtons. This further exception of the committee's ban on foreign equipment is doubly curious considering that adequate French equipment was available for the job and that Otis had requested Worthington pumps but was refused. Apparently Edoux's prestige was such that he could dictate what he wanted. Another explanation is that as the tower neared completion the Exposition committee grew so sick of the whole question of the tower's elevators that it became increasingly lenient. Engineering experts on the committee's technical council knew little about elevator technology. Neither did the tower's builder, beyond what he could understand in terms of basic mechanical engineering. Eiffel could guarantee on his own authority that his structure would stand. He could not say with the same certitude that none of the elevators would fall, for he had had no hand in designing them. But he was satisfied that the makers' calculations were right, and the responsibility was his. The committee, we may imagine, kept its fingers crossed.

It was time, in early 1889, to put the finishing touches on the tower. Most of the work went into the first level, where the majority of visitors were expected to stop. Open in the middle, the platform consisted of a rectangular promenade area 930 feet long and nine feet wide, sheltered by nine decorative arcades on each side. Here the public would get its first panoramic view of the city and the Exposition, buy souvenirs and eat a meal at one of the tower's four restaurants, each with a different style and cuisine. Brébant, one of the best restaurants in Paris, opened a branch, with a Louis XV décor, on the tower; its terrace offered one of the best views of the Exposition grounds. Opposite it, fac-

99

Left: *On completion of his tower, Eiffel poses with his son-in-law, Adolphe Salles, on spiral staircase leading from third platform to flagstaff.*

ing the Trocadéro Palace across the Seine, was installed an Alsace-Lorraine restaurant; a Russian-style restaurant faced the center of Paris, and on the fourth side was an Anglo-American establishment.

On the second platform workers were setting up a printing press and editorial room for *Le Figaro,* which would publish a special daily edition covering Exposition activities. Here gastronomy was limited to a bar and a pastry shop. The center of the platform was taken up by the Edoux elevator.

Above, the octagonal third platform was being completely enclosed behind glass windows to protect visitors from wind. A short spiral staircase led up from the third platform to a small apartment, including rooms reserved for scientific experiments, that Eiffel had built for his own use. On the small balcony running around the platform, tracks were laid to carry two high-powered spotlights with a range of seven miles, which could be wheeled around to illuminate different monuments in the city for the pleasure of those on the tower. At the tower's summit there was also a beacon that had a range of nearly 120 miles and could be seen by observers from the spires of the cathedrals of Chartres and Orléans. The beacon's electric lamp was enclosed by a cylinder containing colored prisms giving off blue, white and red flashes as they revolved every ninety seconds. Protecting the tower at the top were the eight lightning rods connected to iron conduits three inches thick running down the east and west piers to ground deep in the earth.

All along its height, the tower was getting a coat of reddish brown paint named Barbados Bronze. Deep-toned on the lower piers, the color was progressively lightened until it was nearly pale yellow at the top, accentuating the visual impression of height. At the first level Eiffel decided to paint the names of seventy-two French scientists who had distinguished themselves since 1789. This "invocation of science," as he called it, reflected his worry over accusations that the tower was useless and

100

Eiffel's apartment on the third platform as it looks today.

wasteful. The names of Ampère, Daguerre, Gay-Lussac and more than sixty others in gilded letters two feet high all around the tower would, he hoped, convince critics that the thing had a nobler purpose than to titilate the masses. Eiffel was not only pained, as Le Corbusier said, by a lack of recognition of his aesthetic sense; he seems to have abhorred the idea that his thousand-foot tower might be considered fundamentally frivolous. He attempted to lay to rest any such notion during an address to a professional society in Paris in late February. "Besides its soul-inspiring aspects," he contended, "the tower will have varied applications for our defense as well as in the domain of science." Heedless of protesting too much, he went on to list what he saw as the tower's potential uses:

101

Strategic operations — In case of war or siege it would be possible to watch the movements of an enemy within a radius of 45 miles, and to look far beyond the heights on which our new fortifications are built. If we had possessed the tower during the siege of Paris in 1870, with its brilliant electric lights, who knows whether the issue of that conflict would not have been entirely changed?

Meteorological observations — It will be a wonderful observatory in which may be studied the direction and force of atmospheric currents, the electrical state and chemical composition of the atmosphere, its hygrometry, etc.

Astronomical observations — The purity of the air at such a height, the absence of mists which often cover the lower horizons in Paris, will allow many physical and astronomical observations to be made which would be impossible in our region.

Scientific experiments may be made, including the study of the fall of bodies in the air, resistance of the air according to speed, certain laws of elasticity, compression of gas and vapors, and, using a large-scale pendulum, the rotation of the earth. It will be an observatory and a laboratory such has never before been placed at the disposal of scientists.

As time went on, the tower *would* come to be taken seriously, occasionally by scientists but more often by painters, poets and intellectuals who found in it an object of contemplation or a means of transcending the ordinary. Probably the first person to record the spell that the tower could cast on the unwary was a reporter from the solemn daily, *Le Temps,* who visited the monument in March 1889 as work was being finished. "Was it simply the weather that day, or do visitors always feel it?" he wondered:

Whichever the case, an indescribable melancholy, a feeling of intellectual prostration took hold of me. At a height of 350 feet, the earth is still a human spectacle; an ordinary scale of comparisons is still adequate to make sense of it. But at 1000 feet, I felt completely beyond the normal conditions of experience. At

Eiffel challenges the moon from the top of his "black and gigantic factory chimney" in an 1889 caricature.

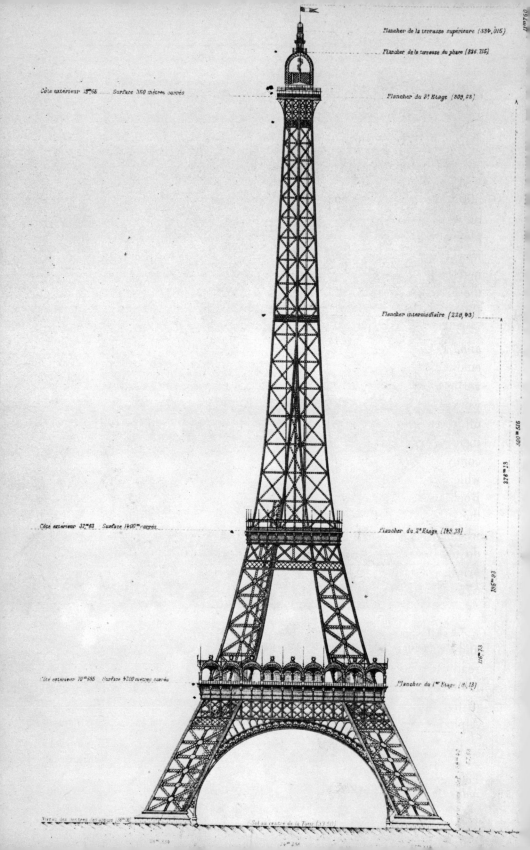

Plancher de la terrasse supérieure (334,015)

Plancher de la terrasse du phare (326.715)

Côte extérieur 15^m65   Surface 350 mètres carrés

Plancher du 3e Étage (309,23)

Plancher intermédiaire (228,43)

Côte extérieur 31^m63   Surface 1400^m carrés

Plancher du 2e Étage (115,23)

Côte extérieur 70^m885   Surface 4200 mètres carrés

Plancher du 1er Étage (57,13)

Niveau des centres des appuis (16^m5)

Sol au centre de la Tour (53,50)

350 feet one can admire the fact that such a puny being as man has accomplished the marvelous work that this infinite city represents; at 1000 feet one no longer understands why man went to the trouble.

At the end of March 1889, the tower stood at its final height of 300.51 meters, or 986 feet. Technicians were still tinkering with the worrisome elevators, but Eiffel's structural work was completed, two years and two months after it was begun. The tower was the world's tallest manmade object by far, making the Washington Monument look stubby by comparison. It would remain the tallest structure until completion of New York's Chrysler Building decades later.

Eiffel's execution had been marked by a deftness unique in the annals of great engineering projects. His clockwork precision had enabled him not only to meet his deadline, but to build the vertiginous structure with the loss of only one life, that of a worker who fell from the first platform while apparently showing off for his girl friend after the bell had sounded ending the working day. Such a safety record was phenomenal compared to other contemporary monumental works like the Brooklyn Bridge, which took some twenty lives including that of its designer, John Roebling, the Forth Bridge, where fifty-seven were killed, and the Quebec Bridge, which cost eighty-four lives. And in a time when cost overruns plagued big projects nearly as much as they do today — the Brooklyn Bridge, for instance, cost twice the original estimate — Eiffel built his tower for exactly $1,505,-675.90, or 6 percent less than the initial budget of $1.6 million.

"Fruit of intuition, of science, of faith, daughter of courage and of perseverance," as Le Corbusier called it, the tower was ready to be christened in that gusty early spring of 1889. Eiffel invited a few dignitaries such as Prime Minister Tirard, members of the Paris Municipal Council and the Exposition's directors, Alphand and Berger, to a simple ceremony that he preferred to

Left: *Diagram of finished tower indicating height of each level.*

The flag-raising ceremony March 31, 1889.

call a *fête intime du chantier*, or work-site party. Promptly at 1:30 P.M. on Sunday, March 31, he led the way up the north pier stairs with his hip-swinging climb. Most of the group dropped out, winded, at the first and second platforms. Eiffel and a few others, among them his veteran colleagues Emile Nouguier and Jean Compagnon, and the President of the Municipal Council, Emile Chautemps, reached the top a bit after 2 P.M. There Eiffel unfurled an appropriately grand French tricolor, fifteen by twenty-five feet and emblazoned with the golden initials R.F., and ran it up the flagpole. Fireworks were set off on the second platform to resemble a twenty-one-gun salute, rather as if the tower were a visiting sovereign.

Eiffel and his party descended, and he addressed the guests and about 200 workers. Toasts were proposed as champagne flowed, an excited Emile Chautemps crying, *"Gloire à Monsieur Eiffel et à ses collaborateurs! Vive la France! Vive Paris! Et vive la République!"* In keeping with the unstated theme of the Exposition of 1889, Eiffel's speech was unabashedly patriotic, from the "great satisfaction" he felt at flying the French flag from the tallest edifice ever built, to the final moral: "You will remember always the great effort we have made in common to show to all that, thanks to her engineers and her workers, France still holds an important place in the world, and that we are always able to succeed where others have failed, to the great honor of France and the Republic." Holding his top hat against the growing wind, Prime Minister Tirard made a brief reply, declaring that Eiffel was being promoted to the rank of officer in the Legion of Honor and that the City of Paris would award a silver commemorative medal to all workers who had been on the site during the last months of construction.

Shortly after the ceremony, a violent spring storm swept across Paris from the northeast, lashing the city with rain, hail and gale force winds. Those who had tarried for a second glass of champagne scurried for shelter beneath the tower's arcades. A thousand feet above the Seine the immense tricolor thrashed and whipped on its lacy iron mast, but held.

SIX

THE PRESIDENTIAL CARRIAGE, a spanking new open landau,
pulled away from the Elysée Palace shortly after lunch. The carriage glided through the gilded gate known, from the strutting
Gallic rooster atop it, as the Grille du Coq, and made its way up
the Avenue de Marigny beneath a profusion of white chestnut
blossoms tall as paschal candles. May 6, 1889, was a brilliant
spring day. A large crowd had turned out along the carriage's
route across the Champs Elysées and into the Avenue Montaigne.
Shouts of *"Vive Carnot! Vive la République!"* were answered
with waves from the landau's three occupants, President Sadi
Carnot, Prime Minister Pierre Tirard and an aide-de-camp,
Colonel Lichtenstein. With a detachment of cuirassiers leading
the way, the little procession crossed the Pont d'Iéna just as the
sixtieth cannon shot of a 101-gun salute rang out. It entered the
grounds of the Paris Universal Exposition, passed under the
colossal arches of the Eiffel Tower, rolled on between colorful
rows of honor guards from France's Asian and African colonies
and pulled up before the ornate iron and glass Central Dome,
official entrance to the fair.

While most of France considered Carnot's appearance at the

President Sadi Carnot arrives for the official opening of the fair May 6, 1889.

Exposition to be the inauguration of the centennial, the significant historical ceremony actually had taken place the day before. The States-General, which had transformed itself into France's National Assembly, thereby effectively ending the reign of Louis XVI, met at Versailles on May 5, 1789. On the eve of the great Exposition, President Carnot had traveled to the château a few miles southwest of Paris and placed a commemorative plaque in the Salle des Menus-Plaisirs, where representatives of the clergy, nobility and commons had gathered. The ceremony was marred, however, for after reviewing troops from the Versailles garrison and watching the spectacle of the château's famous fountains, Carnot was the target of an assassination attempt. The shot fired by an apparently deranged man named Perrin, who considered himself mistreated by the government, went wild. No harm was

109

done except perhaps to the tottering image of the Third Republic, whose fall, one way or another, many considered imminent. The Republic had survived eighteen years, as long as any government in France since the Revolution, narrowly escaping a coup the previous January by the dashing but irresolute General Georges Boulanger. But despite pessimistic predictions by Left, Right and Center, the Third Republic was still on its feet for the opening of the long-awaited world's fair, as was President Carnot.*

The President entered the Central Dome at 2 P.M. to "The Marseillaise" sung by a men's choir accompanied by a military orchestra. Cabinet ministers, members of the Senate and National Assembly, the Paris Municipal Council and other dignitaries filled temporary stands beneath the dome. Others in places of honor were the Exposition's directors, Charles Adolphe Alphand and Georges Berger, next to Charles Garnier and Gustave Eiffel. Directly opposite the podium from which the President delivered his speech sat Madame Carnot, resplendent in a much-admired blue brocaded dress with white lace over dusty pink at the throat, discreetly echoing the national colors. The other ladies attending the official opening were seated on a balcony running around the interior of the dome twenty-five feet above the floor; the gallant correspondent from *Le Figaro* likened them in their light-colored toilettes to "a virtual garland of flowers crowning us."

The diplomatic corps was also present, though with several notable absences. Except for Belgium, the royal courts of Europe adamantly refused to participate in what they considered France's exercise in revolutionary propaganda. Queen Victoria recalled her ambassador, Lord Lytton, to London lest his presence in the vicinity of the fairgrounds be interpreted as endorsement. Similarly, no diplomats represented Austria-Hungary or Russia, and Germany sent only a chargé d'affaires (though the German government later assigned several engineers to report

---

* Carnot eventually did die by an assassin's hand. Three years later, while visiting a commercial fair in Lyons, he was stabbed to death by an Italian anarchist.

110

fully on the Exposition, especially its iron structures). The French government officially ignored the slight by the crowned heads, but the irreverent Paris daily *Le Petit Parisien* gave them the raspberry: "The kings are sulking, as usual," the paper editorialized. "What do we care! The people everywhere are on our side." And the *Manchester Guardian* articulated what the British government dared not admit when it observed, "The Exposition will be seen abroad as a visible sign of the extraordinary recovery of France."

When all were in their places beneath the 213-foot dome, Prime Minister Tirard, in his capacity as commissioner general, formally presented the Exposition to President Carnot. His speech was typical of the genre, reciting difficulties overcome and praising the foresightedness of the government. But if the Exposition itself was an elaborate rite in the industrial liturgy of nineteenth-century secular religion, one passage of Tirard's text could stand as its confident credo:

> Although this splendid result exceeds all hopes, there is nothing in it that should astonish us; progress never goes slowly; new generations constantly replace forces that are exhausted or have disappeared. Science — sovereign power of our century — does not stop the course of its research; every day it penetrates further into the secrets of nature. Steam and electricity have already revolutionized the economic order of the universe — who can tell the prodigies and surprises they still hold for us and our descendants? Inventions, discoveries, improvements succeed each other with stunning rapidity; nothing can resist this enormous push forward. Mills, workshops, factories, stimulated by competition, encouraged by success, undergo constant transformations of which we may be proud, for the result is an abundance of things necessary for life, the lessening of their prices, and consequently the increase of the general welfare.

The President pursued the theme of "a great century which has opened a new era in the history of humanity." After alluding to

111

material and social progress since 1789, he stoutly defended France's right to hold the Exposition, foreign kings and critics notwithstanding: "Our dear France is worthy of attracting the elite of all peoples. She has the right to be proud of herself and to celebrate the economic and political centenary of 1789 with her head held high . . . A century which has seen such miracles had to be celebrated." Carnot's distinguished audience shared his touchiness over the criticisms that had been leveled against the Exposition: the only time they interrupted his speech with applause was when he welcomed foreign visitors and invited them to judge for themselves "the calumnies dictated by blind passions which even the respect due this country could not silence."

The half-hour ceremony over, the President and his entourage began a two-mile walk through the fair's principal attractions. The Exposition of 1889 covered 228 acres in all, including exhibits on the Champ de Mars, the Esplanade des Invalides, along the Quai d'Orsay and in the Trocadéro gardens across the Seine

The colonial pavilions on the Esplanade des Invalides.

from the Eiffel Tower. It was one-third larger than the previous fair in 1878. The main show was on the Champ de Mars, starting with the Eiffel Tower and continuing through the magnificent Palais des Machines, the handsome domed buildings devoted to the fine and liberal arts and industrial displays of all sorts. On the Esplanade des Invalides were military exhibits of the French War Department and the pavilions, in native architectural style, of France's Asian and African colonies. An enormous building fronting the Seine along the Quai d'Orsay housed agricultural and food exhibits. The Trocadéro gardens were given over to horticulture.

While the fair's architecture consisted of the usual potpourri of styles found at such events, it was characterized in the main by the bold use of iron, of which the Eiffel Tower was the most sensational example. In the important pavilions plaster, brick and stone had been banished in favor of iron girders, which were left visible to form the chief element of decoration. As in the impressionist works of the day, which deliberately attracted attention to how a painting was put together, the composition of a structure was becoming the principal visual interest of architecture. In its self-assured use of iron, the Exposition of 1889 was more "modern" than the last great Paris fair in 1900, which despite its permanent legacies of Grand Palais, Petit Palais and Alexandre III Bridge had already turned toward self-conscious academism.

The President's visit was a tumultuous affair, 800 policemen proving inadequate to control the opening day crowd of some 500,000 that streamed through the twenty-two entrances to the Exposition. Carnot was frequently jostled as he moved from one stand to another congratulating and decorating organizers of individual displays. At half-past five, after reaching the Esplanade des Invalides where many of the pavilions were still half-finished, and reviewing the troops from the colonies, a tired Carnot took to his landau for the trip back to the Elysée and left his finance minister to finish the visit. But Paris had only begun to celebrate. The city was festooned with flags, bunting and miniature Eiffel Towers from the National Assembly to the Louvre, from the spires of Notre Dame to theaters, department stores, hotels and the façades of individual apartments. Tricolor banners flew from the scaffolding of the Sacré Coeur basilica, then being built as an expression of national contrition and hope and, like the Eiffel Tower, a reaction to the humiliation of the War of 1870. (Unlike the tower, the ponderous masonry church would take forty-six years to construct.)

When the small cannon on top of the tower sounded closing time at ten that evening, the festive public left the Exposition grounds and lined the Seine to watch a Venetian-style show of brightly illuminated cruise boats slowly plying the river with orchestras playing on their upper decks. Above, the beacon on the Eiffel Tower flashed *bleu-blanc-rouge*, and two powerful spotlights at the top swung around at random to point long white fingers at various quarters of Paris. From time to time the tower's cannon boomed as colored flares were lit on all three platforms, bathing the bronze-colored latticework in sharp, surreal light. The evening climaxed with three gigantic fireworks displays fired simultaneously from the Tuileries, the Pont Neuf and the Ile des Cygnes. The pyrotechnics lasted one hour, regaling the crowds with bombs set off high in the air from balloons, sparkling repro- ductions of Niagara Falls and a flaming bouquet that turned into a recognizable bust of Monsieur le Président de la République.

Meanwhile, the city's cultural elite were at the Comédie Française watching a verse play written in honor of the cente- nary. *The Song of the Century* was a heavy allegorical hymn declaimed by two actors representing Poetry and France. With fulsome exclamations it praised everything the Exposition stood for, and devoted particular attention to its star attraction:

> Clear-eyed Science and active Industry
> Have erected, among the spacious palaces,
> An iron Tower leading to the heavens.
> Unique, strange and truly grandiose spectacle!

A fireworks display on the tower during the Exposition. One of the tower's movable spotlights illuminates the dome of the Palace of Fine Arts, another the monumental fountain.

For another nine days the grandiose spectacle could be viewed but not visited. Eiffel's men were working overtime to put last-minute touches on the tower, but it took them until May 15 to have it in shape for the public, and even then the pesky elevators were not ready. In the first of its special editions composed and printed on the second platform, *Le Figaro de la Tour Eiffel* complained on May 15, "We have put together this number under rather special conditions: in a shack that barely covers our heads,

115

amid carpenters, gas workers, blacksmiths and painters, dizzy from the unaccustomed air, dust and noise and tired by the climb up the equivalent of 36 stories." At 11:50 that morning, Eiffel, with evident relief, signed the guest book kept by the paper in its pocket-size editorial office. "Ten minutes to twelve, May 15, 1889. The tower is opened to the public. At last!"

The line of visitors that had begun forming an hour before started moving up the stairs in the west pier to the first and second platforms. Despite the effort of the climb, during the following week nearly 30,000 persons paid forty cents for a red ticket to the first platform and over 17,000 bought a sixty-cent white ticket for the second. The first elevator to go into service was the clanking Roux Combaluzier model in the east pier on May 26, beating by a week the more sophisticated Otis model in the north pier. The second Otis was ready on June 16. At about the same time the one-dollar white tickets went on sale for the trip to the top in the Edoux elevator.

From then on the tower was, predictably, the most popular feature of the Exposition. Huge crowds often waited hours in line for the opportunity to climb on it, ride on it, eat lunch or dinner on it, buy a souvenir on it, hold hands on it and see from it a breathtaking panoramic view of the Exposition and the world's most beautiful city. In clear weather visibility reached to the Compiègne Forest fifty miles to the northeast, to Château-Thierry forty miles to the east, to Fontainbleau thirty-three miles to the south and far into the rolling plains of Normandy to the west. In theory, at least, the tower could accommodate 10,000 visitors at once: 400 in each of the four restaurants on the first platform, 1000 on the promenade areas of each of the four exterior galleries and 400 on the interior galleries between restaurants, 1500 on the second platform and 500 at the top, plus 2000 going and coming on the elevators and staircases. By the close of the Exposition 1,968, 287 persons had been up the tower, paying the equivalent of $1,142,834.70 in admissions.

116

Some complained about having to pay the same price to climb up as to ride up, but tower officials explained, briefly and irrefutably, that this was "simpler." Visitors averaged 11,000 per day during the Exposition's 176 days, with a record 23,000 on Whitmonday, June 10.

That was also the day Eiffel opened the tower's register, or *Livre d'Or*, to cross-Channel nobility. Whatever Victoria might think of France's centenary, Albert Edward, Prince of Wales and later King Edward VII, and his family visited the tower and took up one large page of the register with their flourishing autographs: Edward's wife, Alexandra, and their children, George, later George V, Victoria and Maud, who became Queen of Norway. Thereafter the tower frequently received VIPs. King George of Greece looked it over on July 22. At his request, there was no ceremony, though personnel at *Le Figaro* chipped in and gave him a guidebook to Paris. On August 1 the Shah of Persia, Nasser Eddim, stopped at the foot of the tower during his tour of the Exposition. Not one to rush into the mysteries of modern technology, he waited on the ground while several of his lackeys made the ascent and returned to give their impressions. The Shah left, remarking only that the elevators made a good deal of noise. But he reconciled curiosity and caution two days later when he returned to climb the stairs to the first platform. He was rewarded with a special edition of *Le Figaro de la Tour Eiffel* printed in Persian, and he took the opportunity to buy two dozen miniature towers and a cane with a tower-shaped handle. In late October Grand Duke Vladimir of Russia accepted a glass of champagne from Eiffel in the engineer's small apartment on the third platform, along with Prince Beloscowitz, Count Weil, and Duchess Josephine Melzi d'Eril of Milan.

Among other notables on the tower that summer were the Khedive of Egypt, the King of Siam, the Bey of Djibouti and of course the President of France, not to mention Buffalo Bill and Tom Tit, a midget clown. Thomas Edison, whose phonograph

118

was one of the most exciting and successful displays at the Exposition, ascended the tower several times. On August 13 he was accompanied by Eiffel's son-in-law, Adolphe Salles, and was photographed with Eiffel on the third platform. A month later he returned to present one of his phonographs to Eiffel (thoughtfully including a recording of the chorus of the Paris Opera singing "The Marseillaise"), which still stands in Eiffel's tower apartment. On this occasion Edison wrote in the register: "To M. Eiffel the Engineer, the brave builder of so gigantic and original specimen of modern Engineering from one who has the greatest respect and admiration for all Engineers including the Great Engineer, the Bon Dieu." Another message, reading "Praise to M. Eiffel with thanks from the Statue of Liberty who owes him her iron skeleton," was signed Frédéric Auguste Bartholdi.

But the toffs had no monopoly on appreciation of the tower. Then as now, the masses responded to it with undisguised glee, appreciating it for what it basically is — a gigantic toy. They were excited when the miniature cannon on the third platform was fired to mark the hour, the ladies cringing prettily and stopping their ears, top-hatted gentlemen assuming an air of martial stoicism. They took the restaurants by storm for the novelty of having lunch or dinner in the sky. They lined up on the second platform for souvenir copies of *Le Figaro de la Tour Eiffel* with the buyer's name quickly printed in the upper right corner with the date. By the thousands they signed their autographs and listed their home towns in the register. Many added their impressions, but for clever word play few matched the amorous wit who wrote:

> *Eiffel, que j'adore la taille*
> *de ta Tour,*
> *Mais, Mimi, combien plus le tour*
> *de ta taille!*

119

Following page: *Fairgoers beneath the tower, 1889.*

Strollers on the first platform.

Smart young things made the ascent in a fanciful dress whipped up for the occasion by a Paris shop in Rue Auber. Known as the *Eiffel ascensionniste*, the outfit featured several superposed collars on the pretext of protecting the adventurous wearer against cooler temperatures at high altitude. Playful young women invented one of that summer's more popular pastimes when they tied messages to gas-filled balloons and released them from the top of the tower. Some of the notes were whimsical billets doux, but others requested that the finder reply. Answers came back from as far away as Belgium, Bavaria and Hungary.

Although the tower was only at the beginning of its career as the symbol of Paris, it was already everyone's favorite touch-

122

stone at the Exposition of 1889. It was not enough to visit the structure and play on it. The tower had to be taken home in one of the numerous forms on sale at souvenir stands all over Paris. Millions of miniature towers, tiny enough to be worn on charm bracelets or large enough to be made into reading lamps, left Paris for thatched cottages in Normandy and the four corners of the earth. An entire meal could be eaten under the sign of the tower with tower-shaped bottle openers, dishes, silverware and salt and pepper shakers decorated with its image, wine and liqueur bottles molded in its form. But the tower inspired more, in those days of craftsmanship, than the gimcrackery found on sale in Paris today. Some of the plates decorated with its image were beautiful specimens of Limoges porcelain. Fine crystal wine glasses, their bases in the shape of the tower, were engraved with its outline in delicate filigree. Huge conch shells were skillfully worked by artisans to produce exquisite cameos of the tower. Full-color pictures of it were enameled on ladies' expensive cosmetic cases and music boxes. Artists and philosophers would later point out the grip that the Eiffel Tower can exercise on the imagination; the public recognized that intuitively in 1889, willingly accepting the tower's reign over the fair. As one speaker at an international banquet during the Exposition put it, "Here we are all citizens of the Eiffel Tower."

That year Paris seemed the center of the universe. News of the great fair had reached practically every point on the globe, and visitors poured into the city, sometimes by the most diverse means of transportation. Most arrived by train, and the Saint Lazare station had been completely rebuilt for the occasion at a cost of $6 million. Its passenger area, the Salle des Pas Perdus, now was 200 yards long and could accommodate thousands of travelers at a time when the boat trains from Le Havre arrived. Next door was the recently opened 380-room Hotel Terminus, which came to be the favorite of American and British visitors.

123

Visitors on the first platform deciding whether to go higher.
The Alsatian restaurant is in background.

But a number of travelers eschewed conventional conveyances to Paris. One anonymous American crossed the Atlantic alone in a small sailboat. On a bet, two Austrians left Vienna in a wheelbarrow, taking turns pushing; they covered the 750 miles in thirty days and won their bet. Another Viennese, a journalist named Moritz Loewy, made the trip in twenty-one days in a rented hackney. One of the most talked about arrivals was that of Lieutenant Michel Assiev, a twenty-five-year-old officer in the Twenty-sixth Regiment of Russian dragoons stationed in the Ukranian town of Poltava. The daring lieutenant made the 1600-mile trip to Paris on two horses, Diana and Vlaga, in thirty days, averaging eleven hours per day in the saddle and losing ten pounds in the process. Paris newspapers gave him a hero's welcome.

By any measure the Exposition was the most successful the world had ever seen. It attracted a paid attendance of 32,250,297 (including an estimated 90,000 Americans), over twice that of the Exposition of 1878, which had been the biggest until then. The permanent population of Paris was swollen by an average of 200,000 persons every day during those six months; the city's businessmen happily estimated at $324 million the amount spent by visitors. Paris was transformed into a swirling vortex with the Eiffel Tower at its center. One of the few not caught up in the gaiety and hubbub was Guy de Maupassant, who continued to sulk:

Beginning in early morning the streets are already full, the sidewalks flowing with crowds like swollen streams. Everyone is heading for the Exposition or is coming back or returning again to it. In the streets, the carriages form an unbroken line like cars of a train without end. Not a single taxi is free, no driver will consent to drive you anywhere but to the Exposition. Besides, the only customers they want are the flashy foreigners. Impossible to find a table in a restaurant, and friends no longer dine at home or accept a dinner invitation at your home. When invited, they

125

accept only on condition that it be for a banquet on the Eiffel Tower — they think it is gayer that way. As if obeying a general order, they invite you there every day of the week for either lunch or dinner.

On the Champs de Mars itself, something over 60,000 exhibitors had spent nearly $36 million to present their displays. Several of the forty-nine countries represented had constructed lavish buildings for their exhibits. The Central and South Americans in particular had made a special effort: Mexico's $1.2 million building was the most expensive, followed by the $1 million Argentinian pavilion. Bolivia, Nicaragua, Chile, San Salvador and Santo Domingo all had their buildings. Paradoxically, many nations representing the most advanced industrial economies of the age did not erect their own pavilions. Germany remained sullenly behind the Rhine, discouraging firms from exhibiting and warning private citizens of a hostile reception if they ventured to Paris for a look at the fair. Mammoths such as Krupp, the Continent's biggest maker of iron and steel products and railroad matériel, and Siemens, a leader in electrical and telegraphic equipment, were thus absent from the Exposition of 1889, although they had been outstanding exhibitors in previous Paris fairs. Great Britain was present unofficially in the form of exhibits by individual firms. But the total outlay for British stands was only around $100,000, about that of Belgium, Portugal, Romania or Japan.

The United States was present officially but did not erect a pavilion. The government allocated $250,000 to defray exhibitors' expenses and named General William B. Franklin, a prominent Union officer during the Civil War and later vice president and general manager of Colt's Patent Fire Arms Company, commissioner general of the exhibit. Due to a certain amount of bungling by Congress and the government, the American show at Paris was not what it might have been, as General Franklin pointed out in his final report. In the first place, Congress dallied for over a year before accepting, on May 12, 1888, France's invitation to participate in the fair. Then, the law that was passed accepting the invitation failed to authorize government departments — except the Department of Agriculture — bureaus and museums to send exhibits to Paris. Other complicating factors were a large centennial exposition in Cincinnati during the summer of 1888, making many firms reluctant to mount another costly exhibit the following year, and apprehension in the United States over possible political instability in France.

These complications, plus the fact that the United States was the last large industrial nation to apply for space, resulted in an American exhibit that was rather shabby compared to those of its better organized European competitors. Altogether the American displays covered some 86,000 square feet, mainly in the Palais des Machines, but its arrangement left much to be desired, as the final report noted bitterly. Promised exhibits failed to arrive, leaving holes in the American section that had to be filled at the last second. As the report stated:

> The resulting fortuitous assemblage of incongruous objects, located in an extensive gallery devoid of interior architectural features and of ornamental installations arranged according to a matured plan, produced anything but an imposing general effect. It can be easily understood how those who judge by the impressions received from the first view of an exhibition, without looking beneath the surface for the merits of the products, may have formed an erroneous estimate of the importance of the United States exhibit.

Americans touring the exhibit were particularly disappointed by the railroad section, a stand that many said looked more like a railroad accident than a display of new equipment. On the whole, General Franklin concluded, "In comparison with the symmetrical arrangement and elegant installations of the French departments, our sections suffered greatly." Such pessimism may have been exaggerated, for when Exposition officials handed out

127

awards at the close, American exhibitors did exceptionally well, winning fifty-five grand prizes, 214 gold medals and 300 silver medals. Grand prizes, for example, went to such diverse enterprises as American Bell Telephone, Thomas Edison, Stetson and Company, Tiffany, McCormick Harvesting Machine Company and that archetypal American business, the Winchester Repeating Arms Company. American supremacy in mechanical engineering was acknowledged by many international observers, including a Belgian jury member judging mechanical exhibits:

> One of the most striking facts that the Exposition of 1889 brings into relief is that, with respect to machinery, American influence is extending more and more and gaining a stronger foothold day by day in Europe. The United States has imposed upon us its forms, its methods of execution, even the organization of work by which more perfect precision is obtained in the production of its workshops, and in the case of steam engines it has imposed its types . . . Does not the difference we find lie in education? In the United States it is free everywhere, everywhere creative and expansive as liberty itself. In Europe it is regulated, powerfully organized, the work of a despotism smacking of the barracks.

Two American exhibits attracted the most excited crowds during the entire six months of the Exposition. One was Thomas Edison's displays of phonographs and electric lighting. Phonographs with recordings and headsets were available for demonstration to the public, and lines formed early each day at Edison's stands in the Palais des Machines. Although one French critic found that "the timbre of voice reproduced is more appropriate to a Punch and Judy show, and the static makes all charm and illusion impossible," most who tried on the headsets were enthusiastic. "The phonograph faithfully reproduces the human voice," wrote another visitor to the stand, "clearly pronouncing even the most difficult diphthongs." The press announced solemnly that

128

the French Academy planned to create a library containing the voices of all its august members: "One of the most prodigious advances of the future will be the ability to make the dead speak."

The other popular American display, though not actually an exhibit, complemented Edison's by presenting the nonindustrial face of the United States. Billing itself on posters all over Paris as *"L'Attraction la Plus Grande du Monde,"* Buffalo Bill's Wild West Company arrived at Le Havre on May 11. Just who William Frederick Cody was needed some explanation for Parisians. One daily undertook to clear up the matter with a highly imaginative thumbnail portrait of him: "Buffalo Bill, who will be our guest during the Exposition, is in a sense the Robinson Crusoe of the New World. Adventurous to excess and brave to the point of recklessness, he succeeds in his audacity and his whims through really extraordinary strength and suppleness. He is the descendant of a most aristocratic family." Costarring Annie Oakley, billed as "Queen of the Rifle," the company of cowboys and Indians set up on the western outskirts of the city and gave its first show on May 18 for a bemused President Carnot. Thereafter the show was packed afternoon and evening for the duration of the Exposition. On their off hours the members appear to have done their share of sightseeing: the third person — and first American — to sign the register on the Eiffel Tower on May 15 was a gentleman named A. S. Hayne, who listed his home town as Fort Worth, Texas. (The first two: Alfredo M. Tillo, an Argentinian, and J. D. Gaite, from England.)

Although the Eiffel Tower was the most spectacular structure at the Exposition, it was not actually the largest. That title went to the Palais des Machines. A palace of iron and glass erected to the glory of steam power, of screws and gears and pistons and flywheels, the vast hangar had a nave 377 feet wide, the broadest space ever covered by a single span of roof until that time. With

129

Interior of the Galerie des Machines. Platform of the rolling bridge that carried spectators from one end of the hall to the other is at left.

a length of 1380 feet and lateral wings extending off the main hall, it enclosed nearly fifteen acres. Twenty gigantic curved girders arched 160 feet above the exhibition floor to support a glass roof. Impressed observers groping for comparisons found that Paris' Vendôme column could stand in the Palais and leave twenty-three feet of space above Napoleon's head; if the building were turned into an annex of the nearby Ecole Militaire after the Exposition closed, there would be room to exercise 1200 cavalry horses at a time. Total weight of the iron in the structure was 500 tons more than in the Eiffel Tower.

At the Paris Exposition of 1889 as at the industrial fairs that had preceded it, the Palais des Machines was the heart of the

130

matter, a cornucopia filled with the most ingenious products of the industrializing world. Exhibits ranged from machine tools to mining machinery, from spinning and weaving machines to electrical and railway equipment. Most of the machines were in motion, powered by thirty-two steam engines providing over 5000 horsepower through miles of underground conduits. Visitors who desired an overall view of this roiling sea of elbowing tie-rods and spinning whirligigs could ride on an electrically powered rolling bridge spanning the central nave. Two hundred spectators could stand on the bridge as it moved slowly from one end of the Palais to the other.

Among the exhibits was the world's first gasoline-powered automobile, a Benz. The car was still largely a curiosity for most visitors, whereas the variety of unicycles, bicycles and tricycles on view captivated a public in love with what Parisians called *la petite reine*. A French company displayed its ambitious new steam tricycle, capable of attaining considerable speed and of climbing steep grades despite its weight of 400 pounds. Exhibits of typewriters attracted almost as many eager spectators as Edison's phonograph; the relative merits of keyboard machines such as the Remington and single-key models like the Mercury created lively debate around the stands.

But while there was far more diversity in design of similar products than exists today, the series of international expositions held from 1850 to 1900 began the move toward standardization. "Each nation," one observer noted, "gradually losing its prejudices, has adopted the improvements which have enabled another to take the lead in any particular direction, whether in matters of practical importance or of good taste. A general uniformity of excellence, amounting indeed to a certain lack of individuality in the design of the machinery of any one class, was a marked feature of the Exposition of 1889."

The grand Palais des Machines itself succeeded almost too well in its awe-inspiring dimensions. It had ample room for the fair's plethora of industrial exhibits, but critics remarked that its immensity dwarfed its contents. Compared to the building, even the largest machines appeared insignificant. Moreover, if the glass roof admitted an admirable amount of daylight, its panes had a regrettable tendency to break during expansion and contraction of the iron framework due to temperature changes, and occasionally showered the floor with sharp shards. The hall's designers had assumed that the great volume of enclosed space would make forced ventilation unnecessary. But with midsummer sunlight streaming in, heat on the exhibition floor often became almost unbearable in the afternoon. Thus most of those attending the Exposition were glad, once they had done their duty by compound locomotives and Westinghouse air brakes, to turn to more frivolous matters.

Next to viewing the fairgrounds from the Eiffel Tower, the best way to get a quick survey was to board one of the miniature trains that chugged for two miles around the perimeter of the Exposition. Composed of seven cars, including a closed *salon de luxe*, the trains left every ten minutes near the Algerian pavilion on the Esplanade des Invalides and followed the Seine around to the Eiffel Tower, turning left there for a straight run down the Avenue de Suffren to the Palais des Machines. The highly popular little trains carried over six million paying passengers during the fair. A more exclusive means of transportation through the grounds was rental chairs with comfortable wicker seats and spring suspension mounted on large rubber-tired wheels, pushed by uniformed attendants. These were particularly appreciated by *les elegantes* of Paris who disdained to scuff their dainty slippers on gravel paths and wished to appear fresh for lunch at, say, the Russian restaurant on the Eiffel Tower.

This being Paris, eating was one of the more important activities connected with the Exposition. A tour of the huge food and agriculture exhibit hall, running for nearly a half mile along the Quai d'Orsay, was a must for most visitors. Food products

132

from all over the world — including English bread, which the French appear to have found intriguing although a bit heavy — were on display, along with the latest model machines for slicing, grinding and mixing food. In terms of size, the most impressive single exhibit was a Gargantuan oaken wine barrel sent over from Epernay by one of France's biggest champagne makers. Its head carved and gilded with rococo extravagance, the barrel contained the equivalent of 200,000 bottles. Ten pairs of oxen had drawn it to Paris on a route carefully planned to avoid narrow bridges. But food was not merely to be contemplated at the Exposition. When 18,000 mayors from the French provinces gathered in one wing of the Palais des Machines for a banquet hosted by the government, they put away a meal that would have daunted Rabelais: soup, trout, cold beef filets, truffled hen, young roast turkey, spring salad, frozen soufflés, chocolate cake and rum baba, accompanied by Madeira, two Bordeaux vintages, one Burgundy, coffee and liqueurs. The fifty-odd restaurants, cafés, snack bars and buffets on the fairgrounds were crowded daily to overflowing, and forewarned families brought along well-filled hampers. Picnics of cold meat, cheese, fruit and wine on the lawns and steps of exhibit halls soon became one of the fair's popular impromptu activities. More exotic gastronomic attractions were available in the Exposition's Rue du Caire, a facsimile of a Cairo street complete with bustling bazaars, beggars demanding baksheesh and donkey drivers beating their animals. The street's cafés offered strong, bitter coffee and gummy cubes of Turkish delight along with undulating belly dancers.

This was in fact one of the most exotic world's fairs ever held. France's colonial empire extended from Southeast Asia to West and North Africa. The colonies' pavilions lining the east side of the Esplanade des Invalides formed a colorful, jumbled world apart. Strollers had their senses agreeably assaulted by the smell of Oriental spices and North African couscous, the

133

sound of Senegalese tom-toms, Polynesian flutes and Annamite gongs, the sight of Moslem minarets and Cambodian temples. In the bazaars of the large Algerian and Tunisian pavilions craftsmen fashioned jewelry, finely tooled leather and brightly colored tapestries. Nearby, nubile young women from Java and Tahiti performed native dances with an authenticity that some prim observers found scandalous. Indeed, presence at the fair of thousands of natives from the colonies worried self-appointed monitors of public morality. A correspondent from one very proper Paris newspaper wrote, "I must demand supervision of these natives whose loose morals border on licentiousness. It appears that their behavior is due to an excess of innocence on their part. But they would be just as interesting if they were a little less innocent."

Art had its place at the Exposition. The liberal arts and fine arts pavilions, handsome buildings roofed with glazed tile domes nearly 200 feet high, faced each other along the Champ de Mars. Beneath the dome of the Palais des Arts, however, wall space was generally limited to the works of those painters who adhered slavishly to the clichés of academic style. The jury that decided which works would be admitted was headed by Ernest Meissonier and Adolphe William Bouguereau, two prominent members of the academic school that favored photographic realism and syrupy subjects. Most Parisians, unaware of or frankly hostile to the wind of creative change called impressionism, still doted on flowery hymns to spring, Virgins surrounded by rosy cherubs, a fleshy Bacchus in his cups. Another year would pass before a young painter and critic named Maurice Denis boldly wrote in a Parisian art review that "A painting, before being a war-horse, a naked woman, some anecdote or whatnot, is essentially a flat surface covered with colors arranged in a certain order." And despite the fact that no fewer than eight exhibits by impressionists had been held in Paris in the previous fifteen years, their work was

134

represented by only a handful of works among the hundreds of paintings hung in the Exposition's official art pavilion. This omission led to one of the fair's livelier sideshows. Paul Gauguin, one of the most flamboyant impressionists of the day and leader of a small clan of painters who made their headquarters at Pont Aven in Brittany, went to a large café next to the Palais des Arts and offered to decorate it with nearly 100 paintings and drawings by the Pont Aven group. The wall mirrors the owner had ordered had not arrived in time for the Exposition, so he agreed to hang the paintings. Gauguin named the exhibit the Impressionist Synthetist Group, strung a blue and white banner across the café entrance and pasted posters all over Paris advertising the show. The enterprising café owner hired an all-women's violin ensemble to serenade the crowds as they streamed in to be titillated by the revolutionary inversed perspectives on the walls. Success of his rump exhibit assured though the press ignored it, Gauguin spent most of his time indulging his taste for South Pacific dancers in the Exposition's Javanese village. In 1891, he left for Tahiti.

Meanwhile, revolutionaries of another sort were meeting in Paris. Of the seventy-odd international conferences held in conjunction with the Exposition covering subjects from criminal anthropology to medical jurisprudence, lifesaving to ballooning and carrier pigeons, the most significant in its long-term repercussions was the founding congress of the Socialist Party's Second International. Several of the objectives agreed upon by the congress — radical notions at the time — have become part of normal industrialized economic and political life: eight-hour workdays, universal manhood suffrage and selection of May Day as the occasion for a demonstration of working-class strength. Interestingly for disciples of Marx, May Day was proposed not by European ideologues but by the pragmatic American Federation of Labor; the motion was passed despite objections by the German delegation that it was too provocative.

Monumental fountain in front of the main entrance to the Exposition. Chairs at right and left accommodated crowds at evening shows of luminous fountains.

Electricity, just beginning to replace the melancholy yellow gaslights along Paris streets, made the Exposition of 1889 the first world's fair to remain open in the evening. The Eiffel Tower was illuminated by thousands of electric bulbs; the pavilions and gardens on the fair grounds were garlanded with strings of lights. And at nine every evening began one of the fair goers' favorite shows, a brilliant display of luminous fountains. Folding chairs surrounding the monumental allegorical fountain representing "France Steering the Ship of Progress" were occupied hours before the first jet of vibrantly colored water shot sixty feet into the air. Located squarely in the middle of the Champ de Mars between the Eiffel Tower and the Central Dome, the fountain by day was a triumph of pompous academic sculpture. France, a plump, winged lady raising a torch in her right hand, steered the ship of the Republic, with a crowing Gallic cock on its prow, as lissome young things named Science, Art and Progress cheered her on. At night, all this could be overlooked as columns, curtains and corollas of water spurted from nozzles in a reflecting pool 120 feet long and fifty feet wide. Illuminated from the pool's bed by a complex system of electric lights behind colored lenses, the fountains seemed to hurl glowing rubies, diamonds, pearls, sapphires and emeralds at the evening sky as crowds marveled at this latest scientific gadget. The show went on for twenty minutes, nozzles and lights shifting and combining to produce changing patterns of ever more grand effect. The spectacle was repeated twice again every night. Few of the millions who applauded this further evidence of lively French genius were aware that it was the creation of the British firm·of Galloway and Sons, who previously had built similar fountains in London, Manchester and Glasgow.

The Paris Exposition of 1889, scheduled to close officially on October 31, stayed open an extra week to satisfy popular demand before it was finally turned over to the demolition crews

137

on November 6. The French government, thoroughly pleased with its centennial, held a formal closing ceremony on Sunday, September 29, at which it awarded grand prizes, medals and diplomas to some 33,000 exhibitors. The centennial's economic and political themes had been well served by the fair, President Sadi Carnot said in his closing remarks, adding, "Here has been shown the glorification of the work of 1789, the emancipation of industry, and a complete picture of one of the greatest economic and social revolutions of humanity." Prime Minister Tirard took the occasion for a final pot shot at the Exposition's critics: "This coincidence of the celebration of the centennial of the Revolution of 1789 with a great international exposition is not, then, as seems to have been believed, a sterile political manifestation, but is really the demonstration of the power and vitality of a free nation . . ." The Third Republic, which a few months before had seemed on the verge of a Boulangist coup, was stronger than ever. A general election the previous Sunday had strengthened its hand: only forty-four Boulangists won seats in the 550-member National Assembly. Many observers were convinced that this new "power and vitality" was due in good part to the overwhelming success of the Exposition. It had convinced the French themselves that a republican government was viable after all. Even Maupassant grudgingly acknowledged that the fair "has shown the world, just when it needed to be shown, the strength, the vigor and the inexhaustible wealth of that surprising country: France."

On the international scene too, France had made her point. Henceforth she would be taken seriously in the industrial world. A German journalist, returning home after visiting the fair, wrote:

> We have been only too inclined to see French industrial spirit in decline. That is a fatal error, as this Exposition proves strikingly. The giant constructions on the Champ de Mars and the Esplanade des Invalides with their huge and richly filled galleries

138

are proof that the French capacity for work has not been idle for a single moment, and that this nation is firmly resolved to reconquer its preponderant place in world markets.

Commissioner General William B. Franklin of the American exhibit was similarly impressed. In his final report he frankly declared his admiration for what France had managed to bring off:

> Everything connected with the Exposition convinces an intelligent observer that the nation which could thoroughly organize so grand a work must at least be abreast of all modern nations in works of industry and art, and in the ability to organize and utilize the brains and muscles of its people.
>
> Whatever may have been the reputation of France before the Exposition in these respects, it must be acknowledged that no other nation in the world could at this time have equaled France in its display of modern fine arts or could have exceeded it in any other department of the Exposition; and it is certain that no such great result, due to ability of administration and energy of purpose and to the enormous wealth of objects — the results of industry and art — has ever been attained by any other nation or can be surpassed in the near future.

But the Exposition's most lasting legacy was neither economic nor political; rather, it was an utterly superfluous thousand-foot iron tower. Fortunately the tower stood in Paris, a city whose inhabitants have always recognized the human need of the superfluous. This assured the tower a long and profitable life, certainly longer than anyone — except perhaps Gustave Eiffel — expected in 1889. As for profitability, revenues during the Exposition in addition to the initial government subsidy were sufficient to cover the tower's cost. Eiffel was able to pay off the bondholders that first year of the tower's existence; the tower has been a money-maker virtually ever since.

Well on its way to becoming the world's best-known landmark, the tower had already made converts of most of the vociferous band of writers and artists who had opposed it. The composer Charles Gounod, for example, attended a little party one summer evening in Eiffel's tower apartment, singing and playing the piano until 4 A.M. For such special guests Eiffel kept an autograph book in the form of a folding fan decorated with views of the tower. He himself had proudly written on it, "The French flag is the only one to have a staff a thousand feet tall." Gounod in turn wrote, "The man who could put an army of workers a thousand feet in the air deserves at least a pyramid," and jotted down a tune to go with the message. Intended as a souvenir for Eiffel's daughters, the fan also recorded the change of heart of another protester, Ernest Meissonier, who praised Eiffel's feeling for the changing light of the Paris sky — "an engineer who speaks like an artist." Succeeding folds were covered by such as Frédéric Mistral, the poet of Provence, who scribbled a little ditty, and Thomas Edison. Ten days later Edison would salute Eiffel in the tower's register as a "brave builder." But on August 30, the inventor summed up his enthusiasm for the tower in a phrase of peculiar resonance: "The Eiffel Tower is one of the gravest things done in modern engineering."

SEVEN

BELLE EPOQUE or fin de siècle? Both terms are used to describe the life of Paris following the great Exposition of 1889. Both, to varying degrees, are accurate. Certainly the 1890s were a time of effervescent creativity in the arts, of uninhibited enjoyment of the infinitely variegated pleasures of the capital, of easy assurance that man was master of his fate. Equally surely it was an age of social and cultural leveling, of widespread poverty among the growing industrial proletariat and of bomb-throwing terrorism by radical anarchists. The French revolutionary Saint-Just had said that happiness was "a new idea in Europe"; that often treacherous idea had catalyzed the agitated first century of industrialization and seemed to reach a frenetic climax in the last decades before the First World War.

"I hope you may come to know a time like my youth," wrote Paul Poiret, the great Parisian couturier who was born in 1879, "when people could enjoy the present because they had confidence in the future. The petty worries and annoyances of life had not yet crushed the individual and put a damper on the pleasures of life." Pleasure, intellectual as well as physical, was the operative word of Belle Epoque Paris, then a city of

Caricature of Eiffel published in Punch *at time of
the Exposition.*

two and a half million. "I'd be very stupid not to extract from life what it gives us on the instant," wrote the playwright Jules Renard, adding that when he met a friend on the boulevard he would toss him a new idea rather than simply make small talk, "thus making of what would have been an exchange of banalities, a discussion which enriches the day." Merely to stroll down the *Grands Boulevards* from the Madeleine on past the Opéra was to sample the city's joie de vivre. A glimpse of the latest fashions and an exchange of lively gossip went with a *fine à l'eau* at any of the cafés — as many as 2500 tables lined the sidewalks on summer days — where the worlds of politics, theater and journalism met. The café had been an important Paris social institution since the Second Empire when Tortoni, on the Boulevard des Italiens, attracted a fashionable literary set headed by Alfred de Musset, Alexandre Dumas and the Duc de Morny. By the nineties tastes had changed and Tortoni had to close in favor of the nearby Napolitain and a dozen others including the Café Cardinal, Pousset, Riche, the Anglais, the Grand Café and the Café de la Paix. With a few exceptions such as the Jockey, private men's clubs had never flourished in Paris as in London, but many Parisian males felt the same sort of allegiance to their cafés. It was said that a man would change his religion sooner than change his café, and the poet Jean Moréas thus described the boulevardier's day: "You arrived at your café at 1 P.M. and stayed until seven. You went out for dinner. You came back at nine and stayed till 2 A.M." Cards and dominoes were played in the cafés, letters and poems were written on the marble-topped tables and a moderate amount of drinking went on, but the main pastimes were conversation — the wittier and more malicious the better — and the political intrigue that doomed the life expectancy of a Third Republic government at this time to about twelve months.

On the other side of Paris the Bois de Boulogne attracted the glittering carriages of the *monde* and the *demi-monde*, from the

143

likes of Baroness Adolphe de Rothschild escorted by grooms in cockaded hats to a bejeweled courtesan or "Grand Horizontal," such as Emilienne d'Alençon or La Belle Otero out for a breath of air. Gentlemen settled questions of honor with pistols or swords in the Bois — dueling was not outlawed until after the First World War — often retiring to their favorite café for a drink if, as frequently happened, both participants escaped unscathed. Automobiles were beginning to frequent the wood's earthen paths, on some days to the point where, as one contemporary noted with distaste, "the harsh smell of gasoline obliterates the noble smell of horse manure." Dandies and dilettantes expressed their contempt for the benighted but burgeoning middle class with such extravagances as Boni de Castellane's Palais Rose, a lavish town house in pink marble near the Arc de Triomphe reputed to be the most sumptuous private residence of the late nineteenth century. Like many Paris aristocrats, Boni scorned electricity as a gadget for the nouveaux riches and lit his palace — from the ballroom to the 500-seat theater to the salons and libraries filled with Gobelin tapestries and rare paintings — only with candles.

Maxim's, a new restuarant on the Rue Royale, attracted well-heeled lovers of "le High Life," but one did not have to pay Maxim's prices to have a good time in Paris. Baedeker's guide for 1889 advised that three to four dollars a day was enough to enjoy the city "where luxury is raised to a science." If eighty cents was too much for a bottle of champagne, there was vin ordinaire for pennies per liter. A good restaurant dinner could be had for about thirty cents.

Particularly in the imagination of foreigners, Paris at this time was synonymous with a relaxed attitude toward the flesh trade. Actually prostitution in the city was probably no more widespread or flagrant than in London, Vienna or New York, but streetwalkers and *maisons closes* had become a fixed part of the local folklore in a way that they had not elsewhere. Rumor

144

had it that Paris' licensed brothels were frequented by judges and generals, financiers and government officials, foreign princes and visiting VIPs. Many of the fancier establishments were decorated and furnished with a singular luxury and originality and some became famous. One such brothel featured rooms in different international styles — a Chinese room, a Russian room, an Italian room, an Indian room, a Persian room and so on — and another transformed a chamber into the first-class cabin of an ocean liner, the bed suspended so as to imitate the rocking motion of a ship with its occupants' every move. But in reality the number of registered Paris brothels was in decline, having fallen from 145 in 1870 to seventy-three in 1888.

As the Paris brothel declined, alternative evening entertainment arose in the form of the *cabaret artistique*. Originally semiprivate clubs were small groups of like-minded poets and musicians gathered to sing, play music and recite poetry, cabarets became a fixture of Montmartre night life and by the nineties several had begun to open their doors to the public. They were not for those with tender ears, for the songs and poems ran to Rabelaisian burlesque of bourgeois mores and the mordant political satire of the *chansons rosses*. One of the earliest and most famous of Montmartre's cabarets was the Chat Noir, started by Rodolphe Salis in 1881. The Chat Noir had a small stage where authors recited and acted out their compositions, often accompanied by shadow plays on the wall behind. After it was taken over in 1885 by the flamboyant Aristide Bruant — immortalized with a rakish red scarf thrown around his neck in the poster by Toulouse-Lautrec — the Chat Noir became a favorite of the *Tout-Paris*, which loved to go slumming there even if its fashionable members did not understand the working-class argot used in many of the numbers. Several of the artists who contributed to the Chat Noir's show later became famous, such as Caran d'Ache, who did cutouts for the shadow plays, and playwrights like Alphonse Allais and Maurice Donnay.

145

"As an artist, a man has no home in Europe save Paris," said Nietzsche about this time. The city vibrated like a tuning fork to the most stimulating artistic and intellectual community in the world. All rules, concepts and conventions were open to question and the only absolute value was individual perception, imaginatively expressed. Here *littérature* was something regarded with high seriousness, for throughout the century Paris had been a faithful if exigent muse. The Symbolist poems of Rimbaud, Verlaine and Mallarmé were quoted in the cafés along with couplets from Edmond Rostand's immensely successful new play, *Cyrano de Bergerac*. Marcel Proust, born with the Third Republic in 1871, published his first work in *La Revue Blanche* in 1889; that same year the young André Gide, as yet unpublished, noted in his *Journal* his vision of the ideal literary life in a garret overlooking the roofs of the Latin Quarter, with "at one's feet, before one's table, Paris. And shutting oneself up in there with the dream of one's masterpiece, and only to come out again with it finished." But if Gide's youthful longings seem romantic, Romanticism as a literary movement had long since been discredited by the splenetic poems of Baudelaire and the pitiless social observation of Flaubert, which led to the world-weary short stories of Guy de Maupassant and Emile Zola's harshly naturalistic novels.

It was a beautiful age for the other arts as well. In painting, Seurat and others were re-creating the art. Sculpture was receiving new impetus from the powerful work of Rodin and Maillol. Literature and the plastic arts had their counterpart in the impressionist music of Claude Debussy, whose horizons had been widened by listening to Javanese orchestras at the Exposition of 1889; in 1894 he composed a musical accompaniment to Mallarmé's *L'Après-Midi d'un Faune*. On the lighter side, Paris hummed tunes from *Barbe-Bleue*, *La Vie Parisienne* and other works of Jacques Offenbach. The city's flourishing theater life was dominated by a golden-voiced actress named Henriette

146

Bernard, better known as Sarah Bernhardt. And an entirely new art form was born in 1894 when the Lumière brothers made the first short films. The sciences too blossomed beneath the era's sunny tolerance toward new ideas. Louis Pasteur's monumental work in microbiology — he performed his first audacious inoculation of a human being against hydrophobia in 1885 — bolstered the Belle Epoque's assurance that science would eventually conquer all man's ills. It was also during this period that Marie and Pierre Curie, married in 1895, began their studies of radium that would win them the Nobel prize for physics in 1903.

The financial crisis that had hit the country in the mid-1880s was over, and although France's economic development lagged behind that of the more advanced industrial nations like England, Germany and the United States, the Belle Epoque was generally a prosperous period. Nearly half of France's labor force was still engaged in agriculture, but farm income was good and was protected from competition by high tariffs, and the rapidly spreading railway network insured easy access to markets. France had become a front-rank power in trade, the world's largest exporter of iron ore and the third largest exporter of wheat. It remained the greatest producer of luxury goods such as fine fabrics, perfumes, cosmetics and high-quality wines. Moreover, the increasing national income was untroubled by direct taxation, because the National Assembly voted down proposals for an income tax in 1895 and 1896.

Paris in the nineties was not without its bit of brash Americana, probably best exemplified by James Gordon Bennett. Son of the founder of the New York *Herald*, Bennett was Commodore of the New York Yacht Club and a prominent playboy when he decided to go to Europe in the 1880s after fighting a duel. He soon became a colorful part of the Paris scene, reinforcing his notoriety with such antics as charging up the Champs Elysées one midnight stark naked at the reins of a coach

147

and four. In 1887 he founded a European edition of the *Herald* as a hobby, reminding the editorial staff that he was the only one to be pleased. What it pleased Bennett to read in his paper was news of society, weather, ballooning, yachting, ship movements and animals, especially dogs. To keep his friends who summered in Deauville supplied with the paper he loaded copies into a big red Mercedes racing car, which made the 130-mile trip in two and a half hours — nearly as fast as it can be made today — leaving a goodly number of terrified Norman cows in its wake.*

Such was the stuff of Belle Epoque Paris. Like the Eiffel Tower it had engendered, the era was frivolous, but behind the frivolity lay imagination, talent and a high degree of competence. As Barbara Tuchman summed up this grandly ambivalent age in *The Proud Tower:*

> Its inhabitants lived, as compared to a later time, with more self-reliance, more confidence, more hope; greater magnificence, extravagance and elegance; more careless ease, more gaiety, more pleasure in each other's company and conversation, more injustice and hypocrisy, more misery and want, more sentiment including false sentiment, less sufferance of mediocrity, more dignity in work, more delight in nature, more zest.

But even "the permanent glamour of France," as one English observer described French cachet in the nineties, could not conceal the travail of fin de siècle Paris. Beneath the gaiety and charm ran violent cross-currents that rent French society with passionate political, economic and religious disputes, while confused moral standards led to public cynicism and corruption on a heroic scale. By one indirect measure, public confidence

* The *Paris Herald* also had a serious side. It was the first newspaper in Europe to be equipped with linotype machines, and later was the only paper in Paris to continue publishing during the summer of 1914 as the German Army advanced on the city. Its descendant, the *International Herald Tribune*, published in cooperation with the *New York Times* and the Washington *Post*, is one of the most informative dailies in Europe.

appears to have peaked in 1889, for that was the last year the French birth rate exceeded twenty-five per thousand; this figure plummeted to 17.5 by 1909. Indeed, the nineties got off to an inauspicious start when Paris was hit, in 1890, by an influenza epidemic, which some French scientists theorized originated in dust compounded of Yellow River mud and the bodies of drowned Chinese, there having been disastrous floods in China in 1888. Paris also experienced an unusually severe winter that year. Crowds of poor flocked to the snow-covered Champ de Mars where temporary shelters were constructed, open fires were kept fueled for warmth and cauldrons of free soup simmered continuously.

Politically, the Third Republic remained a hazardous balancing act, the result of reluctant agreement among opposing forces to make the best of a bad thing. It had to get along without a constitution, for there was so little consensus at its founding that one could not be formulated; a series of ad hoc constitutional laws formed its legal basis. The threat from the Left to France's third experiment in democracy was exceeded only by the determination of the Right to overturn the Republic in favor of a monarchy. The aristocrats despised the bourgeoisie, which feared the peasantry and industrial proletariat. The Catholic Establishment spurned Protestants, and rabid nationalists openly professed their hatred of French Jews. Small wonder then that from its founding in 1871 until 1879, when the Chamber of Deputies and Senate moved back to Paris from Versailles, there were twelve governments, or that there would be fifty by the beginning of the First World War.

Discontent with the bleakness of industrial society and abuses of unbridled capitalism ran high among workers and intellectuals, spawning anarchist terror bombings in cafés, business offices and the Chamber of Deputies itself from 1892 to 1894. Paris lived in such fear during this period that if a streetcar had minor mechanical trouble or a bit of scenery fell at a

149

crowded theater panic and cries of *"Les anarchistes! Une bombe!"* quickly ensued. The anarchists menacingly sang, "Dansons la Ravachole/Vive le son/De l'explosion." Detailed directions for terrorist tactics were listed in such pamphlets as the *Manual of the Perfect Dynamiter*. This wave of terrorism culminated in the assassination of President Sadi Carnot in June 1894, which led to passage of special laws for suppressing anarchist publications and allowing instant searches and arrests of suspects. Carnot's successor, Casimir-Périer, resigned six months later in frustration at the powerlessness of the presidency, and *his* replacement, Félix Faure, lasted only four years before expiring, in perfect fin de siècle style, in the arms of his mistress at the Elysée Palace.

Scarcely had the anarchist violence passed when a Jewish army captain named Alfred Dreyfus was unjustly convicted of selling military secrets to Germany, throwing France into one of its worst political convulsions since the Revolution. Dreyfus, an artillery officer on the French General Staff, was convicted in 1894 by a court-martial held in camera on the basis of fraudulent evidence, and was sent to Devil's Island off the north coast of South America. The army's action was sustained by the atmosphere of virulent anti-Semitism stemming from the French bourgeoisie's fear of Jewish control of the nation's financial life. Racism was nurtured by hate literature, such as the widely read *La France Juive* by Edouard Drumont, a journalist, published in 1886. Drumont founded the National Anti-Semitic League in 1889 to combat "the clandestine and merciless conspiracy" of Jewish finance, and in 1892 started an anti-Semitic newspaper, *La Libre Parole*. But despite Drumont's propaganda and the army's best efforts to close the case, doubts lingered about Dreyfus' guilt because no convincing motive could be found for his alleged crime. The Dreyfus Affair burst on public consciousness in January 1898 when Emile Zola, then at his height as France's most prestigious author, published an open

150

letter to the President entitled *J'Accuse,* in which he spelled out the arguments against the army's handling of Dreyfus. Public opinion divided sharply along religious and political lines, with Protestants, Jews, freemasons, anticlericals and enemies of the Republic calling for a revision of the judgment on Dreyfus, and the army, Catholics, monarchists and nationalists defending the conviction. Tried and convicted of libeling the army, Zola fled to England, but the tide had turned. Dreyfus was returned from Devil's Island in 1899, and after twelve years the poisonous affair was finally over when he was vindicated by an appeals court in 1906.

Cunning and connivance were the basic components of the tacitly accepted modus operandi of fin de siècle Paris. The highest institutions in the land were besmirched with corruption; for example, in 1887 the son-in-law of President Jules Grévy was caught trafficking in official decorations from his office in the Elysée Palace, forcing Grévy to resign in shame. Three years later, several Paris municipal councilors were involved in murky transactions in municipal bonds, which they had acquired at bargain prices and sold at premium rates. As a consequence of inadequate banking and financial laws and public gullibility about get-rich-quick schemes, France was racked by one sensational financial scandal after the other. One of the first big scandals hit in 1882 when the Union Général bank suspended payments, resulting in a financial crash that wiped out the savings of thousands of people, including many priests and bishops; the bank had the declared objective of promoting the interests of Catholics, and Pope Leo XIII had himself invested several hundred thousand francs in it. After the collapse, the Austrian ambassador to Paris, Count Wimpffen, who had been implicated in some of the bank's ventures in Austria, shot himself dead in a Paris kiosk. Suicide again resulted when Denfert-Rochereau, governor of the Comptoir d'Escompte, killed himself in 1888 after the bank attempted to corner the copper market and failed.

The scandals finally culminated in the most spectacular crash of all, which involved hundreds of thousands of bondholders and compromised nearly 150 members of the National Assembly, dozens of newspapers, several important financial promoters and the builder of the recently completed thousand-foot tower: the Panama Affair.

As general contractor for the Universal Interoceanic Panama Canal Company since December 1887, Eiffel and Company had plunged ahead with work at a pace that put it well in advance of the schedule called for in its contract with Ferdinand de Lesseps. Steady progress was being made in cutting through the rocky, 300-foot Culebra range. Eiffel's patented canal locks — "a mechanism so simple that a child could set it in motion" — were being constructed in Brittany. Lesseps finally having made the decision to build the Panama Canal in the form of a gigantic, ten-lock liquid staircase — Eiffel's idea to begin with — the project seemed to untangle itself for the first time. But that decision came too late. Not even a great engineering plan could save Lesseps from his naiveté, self-delusion and financial ineptitude.

On December 14, 1888, the Panama Canal Company filed for bankruptcy. It had begun operations eight years before with far less capital than experts had predicted the job would require, and since that time Lesseps and his advisers had consistently and probably deliberately underestimated costs. The company had attempted six public bond issues with diminishing success, the last in December 1888 being less than half subscribed. Lesseps' promise that "the day will come when Panama stock will stand higher than Suez stock" sounded ever more hollow as Panama bonds fell to a fraction of their original price. A billion and a half francs — nearly $300 million — had vanished into the fever-ridden swamps of Panama. After the National Assembly refused by 256 votes to 181 to prorogate the company's

152

debts, resulting in the declaration of bankruptcy, the Civil Tribunal of Paris officially dissolved the company and appointed a receiver in February 1889, one year before the canal was to be in operation according to Lesseps' optimistic predictions.

At first Eiffel refused to believe that France would allow a project so obviously in its national interest to go under. He ordered work to continue at reduced speed in Panama pending a solution to the latest crisis. After all, the company had struggled from one money problem to another since its beginning and had always found a way to stagger on. Eiffel did $1.4 million worth more of work under his $25 million contract before being officially advised by Joseph-Mathieu Brunet, the receiver, that there was no hope of being reimbursed for any future expenses he might incur. Only in the spring of 1889, as the tower was reaching its ultimate height on the Champ de Mars, did Eiffel reluctantly abandon the most ambitious undertaking of his career. He had been betrayed, not by his genius for analyzing an engineering problem and organizing its solution, but by unscrupulous financial jugglers.

In April Eiffel duly requested Brunet, a former cabinet member and a man of integrity, to settle accounts between his firm and the Panama Canal Company. The two decided that there was no need of a long and costly court procedure, and after four months of negotiating they signed an agreement in July 1889, in which both parties declared themselves satisfied and renounced all future claims against each other. The agreement, under which Eiffel as an independent contractor reimbursed the Panama Canal Company $600,000 in advances and turned over all equipment and matériel, was ratified by the Paris Civil Tribunal.

But too much money had been lost and too much political capital was yet to be made for that to be the end of the Panama Affair. Public opinion, egged on by Edouard Drumont in *La Libre Parole*, pressed for an official investigation of the company's failure. After Drumont attacked Lesseps in his book *La Dernière Bataille* as "this man who has lied so shamelessly, who has abused the public with false promises, who has squandered this money in the most disgraceful way," the National Assembly voted in June 1890 to refer Panama to the minister of justice. Things moved slowly at first, but in June 1891 the First Chamber of the Court of Appeal appointed an examining magistrate, Henri Prinet, to investigate the management of the Panama Canal Company's board of directors. Homes and offices of several of the company's officers and Gustave Eiffel were searched and documents seized. Nothing incriminating was found, and when Prinet completed his investigation he recommended against criminal proceedings for lack of evidence of intent to defraud by the company's directors. But public clamor for the heads of those responsible for the crash increased. Piteous stories circulated of life savings lost; for example, a peasant in Bergnac cashed in his pension, sold his father's watch and mortgaged land to raise $600 to buy Panama bonds. The enemies of the Third Republic, from Boulangists to royalists and on through the Rightist spectrum, were rallying once more in hopes of toppling it.

With this kind of heat on his administration, Prime Minister Emile Loubet ordered his minister of justice, Louis Ricard, to begin prosecutions in the case regardless of what the preliminary investigation showed. On November 21, 1892, the prosecuting attorney indicted Ferdinand and Charles de Lesseps, several promoters and Gustave Eiffel on charges of swindling and breach of trust. The same day came the first indication of how far *l'affaire de Panama* would extend across French public life. Jules Delahaye, a Boulangist member of the National Assembly intent upon compromising the government, ascended the speakers' rostrum and stated flatly that some 150 members of the Assembly had accepted payoffs totaling $600,000 to promote the interests of the Panama Canal Company. "There are two categories of Deputies," he charged, "those who took money, those who did not."

"The scandal of scandals in contemporary French history," as a French historian has called the Panama Affair, had burst open. The corruption it revealed in politics, business and publishing shocked even sophisticated levels of public opinion. The scale and diversity of payoffs by the Panama Canal Company to members of the National Assembly and to newspapers to promote its interests, in particular its increasingly unsuccessful bond issues, has never been equaled — the company was found to have spent an astounding $4.4 million in bribes. Suddenly the French language had a new word, *chèquard*, or one who had received payoff checks from the Panama Canal Company. The scandal reached as high as the minister of public works, Charles Baïhaut, and the minister of finance, Maurice Rouvier, and severely compromised the career of one of the most able politicians of the age, Georges Clemenceau.

The fact that several of the company's chief promoters were Jews sharpened the public outcry over Panama. When one of them, Baron Jacques de Reinach, died suddenly and possibly by his own hand on November 20, 1892, and another, Cornelius Herz, fled to England, it became clear that they had been playing for very large stakes indeed. Herz, whose family had moved from France to the United States in 1849 when he was four years old, was a smooth confidence man who had practised quack medicine, pretended to be an electrical engineer on a par with Edison and left a trail of bilked victims from New York to San Francisco. In Paris, where he settled in 1877, Herz ingratiated himself with politicians and businessmen, becoming an important shareholder in Clemenceau's newspaper, *La Justice;* in 1886 he was the first American citizen to receive the Grand Cross of the Legion of Honor, thanks to his connections. But after Jacques de Reinach's death Herz's name was found on two check stubs, each amounting to one million francs. Correspon-

155

dence in Reinach's possession indicated that he had been black-mailed by Herz, who threatened to reveal the degree of corrupt-tion in the Panama Canal Company's operations. Clemenceau's connection with Herz soon became the best-known secret in Paris, but he was a formidable enemy because of his slashing attacks at the podium, his influential newspaper and his well-known fondness for settling differences by duel. In December 1892 an ardent nationalist and author of patriotic poems and plays, Paul Déroulède, rose in the Assembly and asked rhetori-cally who could have been the power behind Herz. "You all know who was this obliging, devoted, indefatigable intermedi-ary, so active, so dangerous," he declared. "His name is on the lips of all of you, but none of you will name him for you fear three things about him — his sword, his pistol and his tongue. Well, I shall brave them all, and name him. He is Monsieur Clemenceau." Clemenceau's answer was to utter "Monsieur Déroulède, you have lied," and to send his seconds to Déroulède with a demand for a duel. Pistols were chosen for the encounter on December 22, not in the Bois de Boulogne but near the Saint Ouen racetrack north of Paris. Despite Clemenceau's undoubted expertise with arms — during practice at a shooting range the day before he had scored twenty successive bull's eyes — both men were untouched after three shots at twenty-five paces. Honor was safe, but Clemenceau was driven from public life by the scandal as voters rejected him for the next ten years. It would be 1906 before "the tiger" would form his first government as prime minister.

It is an index of the moral tenor of the age that when all the investigations were completed, duels fought, trials held and careers compromised, only one man, Baïhaut, was ultimately convicted and sentenced, and then only because he actually con-fessed to taking a bribe. There was no doubt that the company had seriously mismanaged its affairs and done its best to corrupt politicians and journalists, both of which professions showed

156

themselves only too eager to be corrupted. The question concerning Eiffel, however, was whether he should have been implicated at all in the scandal. Public sentiment ran against him because he had made money in Panama. The prosecution's case was that he, along with the board of directors, had misused company funds, and that he held a position of trust and fiduciary responsibility. He contended that, on the contrary, he had merely signed a contract with the company to execute prescribed engineering services, and had indeed rendered these services in exemplary fashion. Eiffel engaged one of the best lawyers in France, Pierre Waldeck-Rousseau, a cool, ironic former minister of the interior and future prime minister (1899–1902) to argue his case. Replying in person to the judge's questions concerning his involvement with the Panama Canal Company, Eiffel stated:

> Monsieur Ferdinand de Lesseps called for my help in terms that touched me. Our relationship had been cool since he had founded the company. I had never believed in a sea-level canal, and I was one of the few who voted against it at the meeting in 1879 at the Geographic Society. Monsieur Ferdinand de Lesseps had never forgotten that vote over the years. Still, I had followed the work on the canal closely. When the difficulties of constructing a sea-level canal became generally recognized in 1887, I was visited by Baron de Reinach, who proposed that I enter into negotiations with the company. Oh, I hesitated. I hesitated a long time.

But, Eiffel explained, his sense of duty to the nation compelled him to attempt to save the project. Nonetheless, at the conclusion of the two-week trial in March 1893, the court found Eiffel guilty of misusing funds entrusted to him while acquitting him of complicity in swindling. He was sentenced to two years in prison and a fine of $4000. Ferdinand de Lesseps — the "Great Frenchman" — his son and two company promoters were sentenced to five years and $600 fines.

The decision was manifestly unjust to Eiffel, who had never had a hand in managing the company's affairs and who as general contractor actually breathed new life into the operation, albeit too late. Only the highly charged atmosphere in Paris after the scandal broke can explain his indictment and conviction. Fortunately, the Cour de Cassation, France's highest court, kept a cooler head and reversed the decision three months later on appeal. The court's reasoning did not give entire satisfaction to Eiffel and the other accused, however, since the reversal was based on a statute of limitations technicality; the court did not judge the ultimate question of guilt. In the emotional ambiance of the affair it would have required a Solomon to render justice, and Belle Epoque fin de siècle France was notably short of men of sure, disinterested judgment. To the detached observer today, it appears that Eiffel did not fraudulently line his pockets at the investors' expense, although his contract did provide him a normal profit margin, but that he must have had some notion of what was being done by the company's directors and promoters. If he was culpable to some extent by association, this surely was mitigated by the fact that he, at least, honestly delivered the goods according to his contract.

Eiffel eventually would be vindicated by yet another court. But before that occurred he had another few yards of post-Panama calvary ahead. The French government still had not given up on the Panama Canal project and encouraged the receivership to form a new company. The receiver and a government-appointed *mandataire,* or attorney representing the old company's bondholders, set out to raise $12 million capital to finance the *Compagnie Nouvelle du Canal de Panama.* They hit upon the idea of suing underwriters and contractors who had made money out of the old company, charging them with ill-gotten profits. After a test case went against one important promoter, banks and underwriting syndicates lined up to buy shares in the new company as fast as they could. The attorney

158

declared that, of the cases against the contractors, the one against Eiffel was the strongest, given the importance of his late role as general contractor. Eiffel got the point and bought $2 million worth of shares in January 1894, thus becoming the new company's largest individual subscriber.

In December of that year Ferdinand de Lesseps, having spent his final six years in semicomatose senility, died without ever becoming aware of the Panama Affair. As the last gusts of the Panama storm blew through the National Assembly, a deputy raised the question of what the Legion of Honor intended to do about the allegations against one of its illustrious members, Gustave Eiffel. The Legion's Grand Chancellor, General Février, responded by convening a committee of inquiry and summoning Eiffel to testify on his role in Panama. Results of the inquiry were presented to the Legion's self-regulating body for decision. In a letter dated April 21, 1895, General Février announced to Eiffel: "Considering that an examination of the conduct of M. Eiffel as contractor for work on the Panama Canal shows that he committed no dishonorable act calling for disciplinary measures, the Legion is of the opinion that there is no reason for action against him."

It was becoming more difficult with passing months to get political mileage out of Panama, but the National Assembly made one more endeavor in July when it passed a motion accusing the Legion of ignoring previous judicial decisions against Eiffel and inviting the government to reorganize it. Three days later General Février shot back a stinging reply pointing out that the Legion was not only fully aware of previous cases brought against Eiffel but also that Eiffel had been declared innocent by the highest court in the land. Because the entire case was technically invalidated by a statute of limitations, there remained the nagging fact that the Cour de Cassation had not passed on the question of whether Eiffel should have been implicated in his role as independent contractor. But the Legion

159

of Honor had gone into precisely this question, Février emphasized, and found Eiffel innocent of any wrongdoing whatever. He furthermore presented to the President his resignation and that of the twelve other Legion officials, including four generals, a vice admiral, the honorary president of the Cour de Cassation and several members of the French Academy. The collective resignation was refused.

After five years of calumny, Eiffel was at last officially cleared of the mud of Panama. The canal that would have been his greatest work, easily surpassing in importance and utility all his bridges and the thousand-foot tower, was finally built by American Army engineers, some of whom were vocal in their admiration for what their French predecessors had accomplished. France's New Panama Canal Company sold out to the United States for $40 million in 1904, yielding to the cold geopolitical logic of what President U. S. Grant had called for as early as 1881: "An American canal, on American soil." Eiffel, reaching for an ever grander achievement to cap his engineering career, had ignored that logic and the evidence of Lesseps' mismanagement in favor of something La Belle Epoque prized more highly — glory. But fate decided that his tower was glory enough.

EIGHT

THE MASTER BUILDER would build no more. No matter how un-
fairly Eiffel had been spattered by the Panama Affair, no matter which tribunal declared his innocence, the stain of scandal
could never quite be removed from French public consciousness.
In the wake of Panama, he chose to retire from his company,
which later changed its name to the anonymous Ateliers de
Construction de Levallois-Perret. This was a harsh reversal of
fortune for Eiffel, but his restless genius demanded outlets.
Panama had not demoralized him; retirement would not mean
withdrawal. In fact, the next three decades were to be among
the most creative of his life, thanks to his imaginative use of the
tower as a test bed.

Shortly after the tower was completed Eiffel made it his
laboratory for many kinds of experiments. One of the first things
he did was to install thermometers, barometers and anemometers
on the third platform in cooperation with France's Central
Weather Bureau. The instruments were wired to monitors in
the Bureau's offices on nearby Avenue Rapp and their readings
published daily. For the first time, French scientists could compare weather conditions at a thousand-foot altitude with those

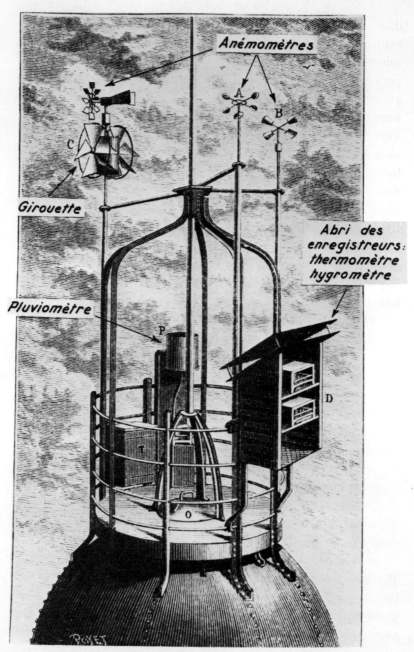

Anémomètres

Girouette

Abri des enregistreurs: thermomètre hygromètre

Pluviomètre

The first weather station at the top of the tower had instruments for measuring rainfall, temperature and humidity, wind speed and direction.

directly below at ground level. Their initial findings seem self-evident today but caused considerable interest at the time in scientific circles burning with the new empiricist fever: temperatures at that altitude averaged exactly 2.3 degrees centigrade lower than those recorded below; temperature variations were less at altitude than at ground level and inversions were frequent, especially during September and October; winds were strongest in January and February, and three times as forceful above as below. Static electricity in the atmosphere was measured, as was the tower's movement at the top caused by wind and temperature variations — five inches' sway in the strongest wind, seven inches' expansion on a hot summer day.

Physiological tests were carried out to determine the effects of altitude on the human organism. The resulting report provokes a smile today despite its determined effort at scientific solemnity:

> On rising by elevator to the third platform, the respiration becomes more ample and easier; the pulse beats faster, then becomes more regular and hardy. At the same time, the subjects experience a feeling of well-being, of general quickening. The satisfaction of being on a plateau with a vast view of the horizon combines with a particularly vivifying air of great purity to produce, especially in women, a psychic excitement that is translated by gaiety, animated and joyous conversation, laughter and the irresistible desire to go still higher — in sum, a general excitement which recalls that provoked by visits to mountain resorts. If the stay at the top is prolonged, there is a remarkable sensation of appetite, while the notion of passing time weakens notably.

The physiologist conducting the experiment, who happened to be a son-in-law of Eiffel's, concluded that ascending the tower was excellent therapy for anemia and dyspepsia, although scientific scruples prompt one today to question whether such eu-

163

phoric results were not due in part to the special nature of the subjects of the experiment — the gay, animated women of the Belle Epoque. A more serious and fruitful line of experiments, however, was to put Eiffel squarely in the avant-garde of several areas of emerging twentieth-century technology, much as his construction techniques with iron represented the forefront of nineteenth-century civil engineering. His mind as alert at seventy as the day he left the Ecole Centrale, he now plunged into basic research in meteorology and aerodynamics, while encouraging the development of wireless telegraphy.

"During my engineering career the wind was always one of my preoccupations due to the exceptional dimensions of my structures," Eiffel explained in his memoirs. "It was an enemy against which I had to struggle constantly. My studies to determine its force led me progressively to investigate other aspects of meteorology and eventually to set up a complete weather station." Eiffel's first meteorological observation post was operating on his property at Sèvres, a few miles south of Paris, before the tower was built. He extended his studies to similar stations at his properties on the Riviera and in Brittany, and to the tower in 1889. Study of weather had made little significant progress since Aristotle had published his *Meteorologica* in the fourth century B.C. When Eiffel suddenly found himself with leisure to devote to the subject, he was dismayed by the obsession of French meteorologists with rigorous but sterile precision as opposed to creative synthesis. Temperatures were recorded to one-hundredth of a degree, but were not put into meaningful context.

As a first step toward synoptic meteorology, Eiffel suggested recording only daily minimums and maximums and putting the figures into graphic form for ready comparison, as was already being done by the United States Weather Service. Appalled as ever by a general lack of system, he found instrumentation woefully lacking in French weather stations, where many observa-

165

Left: *Preparing one of Eiffel's
early aerodynamics experiments
at the tower.*

tions such as cloud cover, hours of sunshine and even wind speed and direction were estimated rather than measured. Eiffel first tackled the problem of instrumentation. He made an effective housing for thermometers and other equipment that gave protection from the elements while permitting a free flow of air. Then he designed improved instruments for observing and automatically recording wind direction and force, insolation and other data. He extended his private weather network to twenty-five stations, including one in Algiers. Finally, to show the way to a hesitant French Weather Bureau, he published at his own expense a series of weather atlases from 1903 to 1912, the first synoptic charts to appear in France and the foundation of modern meteorology in that country.

Simultaneously, Eiffel kept an interested eye on developments in aviation. At the turn of the century flying was little more than a sport for tinkerers and playboys. Ballooning was its most popular form, but the fact that balloonists seldom knew where they would land made it a rather unreliable mode of transportation. The tower became involved in aviation when Henri Deutsch, a wealthy French oil man, created a $20,000 prize in 1900 for the first balloon pilot to take off from the landing field in Saint-Cloud, west of Paris, circle the tower 3.4 miles distant and return within thirty minutes. The challenge was taken up by Alberto Santos-Dumont, Brazilian-born heir to a coffee fortune, who lived in Paris. Santos-Dumont began building powered airships in 1898, and by 1901 he was ready to try the Eiffel Tower run. His first attempt, in July, got him around the tower in forty minutes — too long to qualify for the prize, but still the first recorded flight of a dirigible around a predetermined course. In August he tried again, but after he cleared the tower a propeller became fouled in the rigging and the craft plunged into the Grand Hôtel du Trocadéro across the Seine. Shaken but unhurt, Santos-Dumont built another dirigible, his sixth, and took off again on October 19. This time he made the round trip in twenty-nine minutes, thirty seconds. The prize was his, along with a commemorative gold medal from the Société de la Tour Eiffel. The omen was unmistakable: the tower and its eponymous builder had a role to play in aviation. In 1903, at the age of seventy-one, Eiffel set up a small laboratory on the second platform. While continuing to compile his meteorological atlases, he began a series of separate experiments which, over the next decade, would go far toward putting the fledgling science of aerodynamics on a sound theoretical footing.

Heavier-than-air flying machines were then being built by trial and error out of baling wire and sweat. Steam-powered engines were heavy and unreliable, and no one really knew why a wing, whether on a bird or an aircraft, made flight possible. Early experimenters such as Sir George Cayley in Great Britain had intuitively grasped the nature of powered flight and outlined the general configuration of aircraft by the mid-nineteenth century. But until the basic laws of aerodynamics were better understood there could be no systematic advance in aviation. Eiffel decided that the first question to investigate was the air itself. To find how the resistance of air could be calculated accurately and what forms moved through the air with least effort, he made use of the unique facility his aerial tower provided to experiment with objects in free fall. Eiffel ran a guide wire from his lab, 377 feet above the Champ de Mars, to a point directly below. Objects of differing profiles could then be dropped, trailing a light wire connected to recording devices in the lab to measure speed. Although the drops lasted only five seconds on average, the objects' speed reached ninety miles per hour. By 1905, hundreds of tests with round, square, rectangular and triangular plane surfaces had enabled Eiffel to confirm experimentally the generally accepted physical law that air resistance increased as the square of the surface of the object moving through it. Further, the tests showed that the coefficient figure used by many scientists to calculate air resistance — a figure

167

derived from tests in which objects were whirled on turntables rather than moved straight through the air — was off by as much as 56 percent. Confirmed independently by the great American aviation pioneer, Samuel Pierpont Langley, director of the Smithsonian Institution, the new coefficient was Eiffel's first contribution to aerodynamics.

But the drop tests did not entirely satisfy Eiffel. To prevent his results from being influenced by wind action, he could conduct experiments only during periods of complete calm. Moreover, the range of test models that lent themselves to this method was severely limited. Therefore in 1906 Eiffel built a wind tunnel at the foot of the tower. Powered by the tower's generators, a seventy horsepower electric motor drove a fan system that provided a steady, controlled and turbulence-free flow of air at speeds up to forty miles per hour through a horizontal test chamber five feet in diameter. Although a number of experimental wind tunnels had been built previously — the first by F. H. Wenham in England in 1871 — Eiffel's was the most accurate and soundly conceived by far. Over the next five years this installation became the birthplace of scientific aerodynamics.

Heart of the wind tunnel's equipment was an ultrasensitive set of scales which, when linked to a model of the airplane being tested, measured its overall aerodynamic balance. Other equipment gave precise readings of lift over wing surfaces and efficiency of propellers. By 1911, Eiffel had carried out over 5000 experiments with the wind tunnel, enabling constructors to eliminate a good part of the guesswork in designing their prototypes. In particular, his work led to breakthroughs in two important areas, wings and propellers. As a result of his close study of airfoils, Eiffel proved conclusively that much more lift was produced by the air flowing *over* a cambered wing than by the air striking the wing's underside. Ignorance of this principle by early designers resulted not only in inefficient wing profiles but in numerous crashes when canvas was ripped from the tops

168

Eiffel adjusts a scale-model airplane in his wind tunnel at Auteuil.

of wings by the air's suction force during flight. Propeller design was also made simpler and more effective by Eiffel's discovery that, although propellers might vary greatly in size, they were all essentially similar in their action on the air. They could therefore be designed according to a set equation, which Eiffel drew up in his "Law of Similitude." He also led the way in studying variable pitch and counter-rotating propellers.

With the Champ de Mars neighborhood becoming a favorite residential area of the haute bourgeoisie, complaints began to pour in to city officials about the noisy experiments being carried out at the foot of the Eiffel Tower. The City of Paris informed Eiffel that his wind tunnel violated zoning restrictions, upon which he created another one in suburban Auteuil in 1912. His second wind tunnel was larger and more powerful than the one at the tower, providing an air flow of seventy-one miles per hour through a test chamber six and one-half feet in diameter. With it Eiffel continued his experiments on wings at a more realistic airspeed, finding, for example, the best positioning of upper and lower wings on a biplane and their interdependent lift characteristics. During the following years he studied complete scale models of seventeen aircraft; today their names read like a *Who's Who* of those heroic days of aviation: Wright, Voisin, Blériot, Morane-Saulnier, Bristol, Dorand, Farman, Bréguet, Nieuport among others. Most of the famous Allied fighter planes of the First World War, including the Spad, were tested at the Laboratoire Eiffel before taking to the skies.*

Soon aeronautical engineers in other countries were paying Eiffel the sincerest form of flattery, setting up wind tunnels based on his design in Holland, the United States and Japan. As always, Eiffel scorned secrecy, freely publishing his methods

* The Auteuil laboratory still functions with its original equipment, performing an average of 10,000 hours of experimental work annually. The tunnel's relatively low speed makes it unsuitable today for most aeronautical testing except of small, light aircraft. It is much used, however, for automobile wind-stream tests such as Porsche has carried out there on its racing cars, and for stability tests of high-rise structures like the control tower at Paris' new Charles de Gaulle Airport.

*Eiffel and an assistant conducting an experiment at the
Auteuil wind tunnel.*

and results; his voluminous technical study, *The Resistance of
the Air and Aviation,* appeared in translation in the United
States in 1913. That same year Eiffel was honored by the Smithsonian Institution with America's most prestigious aviation
award of the day, the Langley Gold Medal. The first Langley
Medal had gone to the Wright brothers in 1910. The second and
third were presented to Gustave Eiffel and the American airplane designer Glenn Curtiss on May 6, 1913. The French ambassador in Washington accepted the medal for Eiffel, who
could not attend the ceremony. Alexander Graham Bell in his
capacity as a regent of the Smithsonian made the presentations.
In his speech, Bell noted with some understatement that "The
advance has been much greater in the art than in the science of

aerodromics." In other words, aviators flew by the seats of their pants rather than improving their craft through an understanding of physical laws. Bell continued:

> This eminent engineer, the constructor of the Eiffel Tower, though more than eighty years of age, still continues his studies in his chosen field of labor with all the enthusiasm of youth, and his writings upon the subject of resistance of the air have already become classical. His researches, published in 1907 and 1911, on the resistance of the air in connection with aviation, are especially important and valuable. They have given engineers the data for designing and constructing flying machines upon sound, scientific principles.

Eiffel still had not exhausted his imaginative use of the tower. While he was conducting his meteorological and aerodynamic studies, his agile mind caught a gleam from yet another technological development that seemed to hold promise for the future. The tower was a natural communications post, and as early as 1898 Eiffel encouraged the French radio pioneer Eugène Ducretet to perform experiments with a transmitter on the third platform. Ducretet successfully sent radio messages in October of that year to a receiver in the Panthéon, two and a half miles away, "even in thick fog." When he tried reversing the experiment, he was unable to receive on the tower and concluded that the radio signals were being absorbed by the structure's iron beams. Eiffel demurred, pointing out that similar experiments on naval vessels had succeeded despite the ships' enormous metallic mass.

Marconi's experiments in 1899, in which he sent radio waves across the English Channel, proved the worth of wireless telegraphy to all but government bureaucrats. A young captain in the French Corps of Engineers, Gustave Ferrié, was charged with studying ways of adapting the wireless to military use, but the army could offer no financial or technical support. Eiffel

172

wrote the army in 1903 to proffer the tower as Captain Ferrié's laboratory. The army accepted on the condition that it would incur no expenses, so Eiffel undertook to subsidize the work. The following year Ferrié, working out of a wooden shack and with a single antenna guyed from the tower to a tree on the Champ de Mars, was sending and receiving over distances of 250 miles. By 1908 he had improved his equipment and was reaching Berlin, Algiers, Casablanca and North America; the army, finally convinced, converted the temporary Eiffel Tower station into a permanent facility. In 1911 the station began signaling Greenwich mean time as a navigation aid to ships at sea. During the First World War Ferrié was a general, and his station paid important military dividends. In August 1914, for instance, the tower's receiver captured a radio message from General von der Marwitz, commander of a cavalry division covering the German Army's right flank as it advanced on Paris. Von der Marwitz informed his headquarters that he had run out of feed for his horses and was unable to advance — intelligence that helped convince the French General Staff that the time had come for a decisive counterattack on the Marne.*

In 1920, at the age of eighty-eight, Gustave Eiffel at last began to slow his pace. He had published thirty-one books or monographs covering his landmark projects and the results of his scientific experiments. Had he chosen to wear all the honorary decorations awarded him during his career he would have been bent double beneath a chestful of medals, including the Hungarian Order of Franz-Josef, the Austrian Order of the Iron Crown, the Portuguese Order of the Conception, the Spanish Order of Isabella the Catholic, the Cambodian Royal Order, the Annamite Order of the Dragon, the Italian Order of the Crown, the Russian Order of Saint Anne, the Greek Order of the Savior,

* Following the war the tower housed France's first civil radio station, broadcasting news and music. Television experiments were performed there in 1925, and in 1953 the country's first TV station began operating from the tower.

Eiffel in his study, Rue Rabelais, circa 1920.

the Serbian Order of Saint Sava and the Japanese Imperial Order of the Rising Sun, besides French citations and the Langley Gold Medal. But now as he looked back and began to write his memoirs for his descendants, Eiffel stated unhesitatingly that his greatest work had been the thousand-foot tower, "symbol of force and difficulties overcome." In the twilight of his life he saw it as "this incomparable monument, the tallest ever to come from the hand of man," and insisted one last time that whatever else it might be, the tower was *beautiful,* even majestic, with that special aura of the colossal that defies ordinary aesthetic principles. As a practical man he was happy that his scientific experiments and the radio station on the tower had proved its utility.

Patriarch of a large, prosperous clan, Eiffel lived with his daughter Claire and her husband, Georges Salles, an engineer and close associate of Eiffel's for many years. He made his home in a palatial town house at the corner of the Avenue Matignon and Rue Rabelais, across from the fashionable Jockey Club in the Champs Elysées district, on the site where Paris' Time-Life Building has stood since 1962. He had purchased the large, elaborate house with a severe façade — some of the family jokingly called it "the ministry" — immediately after his triumph with the tower, but had come to live in it only much later. Now its sumptuous Second Empire style, with a roomy graveled courtyard to accommodate several automobiles and an imposing stairway leading to an ornate entrance, suited Eiffel's image of himself. There he liked to reign over his five children, their spouses and the eleven grandchildren at Sunday dinner and family fêtes, the most important of which was on December 15, his birthday. On that day all the grandchildren were expected to present *Bon-papa* with something done by themselves, whether a drawing or a piano recital or a recitation in classical Greek. Kindly but aloof, Eiffel was an intimidating presence to the children.

"He was the perfect figure of a grandfather, with his blue eyes, pink cheeks and white goatee," recalls René Le Grain-Eiffel, son of Laure Eiffel and Maurice Le Grain, who was born in 1889 and had a brilliant career as an automotive engineer. "It would never have occurred to us to try to pull his beard, though, any more than it would have occurred to him to get down on all fours with us. No one ever used the familiar *tu* with him, or for that matter ever saw him in his shirtsleeves." Eiffel remained vigorous physically and mentally well into his eighties, teaching his grandsons to swim and fence, and René Le Grain-Eiffel remembers well that terrible December 15 when his little cousin Jacques attempted to fake it through his recitation of a Greek poem, not knowing that *Bon-papa* retained a working grasp of the language from lycée days.

The times had been good to Eiffel, always a man of his times. He was now immensely wealthy — his company had had an accumulated turnover of more than $14 million by 1890. Besides his Paris town house and his country residence at Sèvres, he owned homes and property in Brittany, Bordeaux, on Lake Geneva and at Beaulieu-sur-Mer on the French Riviera, where he kept a ninety-foot steam yacht. When the humor moved him, he would head for one of these retreats, taking along as many of the family as were free to travel. Although austere by temperament and upbringing, Eiffel liked his personal belongings to reflect his genteel status. Today his study has been carefully reconstructed by his granddaughter, Henriette Venot, at her country house at Salleboeuf, near Bordeaux. There can be seen his monumental oak desk riddled with secret drawers, bibelots such as a delicate white porcelain pipe with tooled silver cap, a book cover of fine red velvet bearing his initials in silver, an expensive amber cigar holder with "GE" marked in gold, several gilt statuettes of Buddha, paying homage to the French bourgeoisie's transient turn of the century enthusiasm for chinoiserie. Eiffel's personal library lines the walls: the leather-

176

bound complete works of Voltaire that had belonged to his father, flanked by Hugo, Labiche, Zola, the Goncourts, much of Maupassant but not *"La Vie Errante"* — whether a deliberate omission one can only surmise.

Eiffel was also world famous, of course, though occasionally he appears to have doubted that his real value was justly appreciated. He was naturally proud of the tower, but then as now that giddy creation often prevented Eiffel's being taken seriously as an engineer and researcher. "I ought to be jealous of the tower," he protested half seriously. "It is much more famous than I am. People seem to think it is my only work, whereas I have done other things, after all." At such moments he was glad of even the simplest manifestation of interest in his other work. Le Corbusier recalled once that he had telephoned Eiffel in 1923 to request a photo of the Garabit viaduct to illustrate an article he was writing. The young architect was pleasantly surprised by the receptive amiability of the old gentleman who was reputed to be so distant and crusty: "Eiffel's voice was soft. He was affable, even friendly. He was enchanted by my juvenile admiration."

Eiffel's main work now was writing his memoirs, in reality a brief outline of his life and career intended only for the family archives. In line with the traditional French discretion about family matters, he deliberately refrained from publishing the work, distributing five mimeographed copies to his children after he finished it in September 1923. On December 27 of that year Gustave Eiffel died peacefully at the age of ninety-one in his mansion on Rue Rabelais.

Si monumentum requiris, circumspice. That epitaph would be as apt on the Eiffel Tower as it is in Christopher Wren's Saint Paul's Cathedral. Indeed, the tower is Eiffel's only proper monument, for contrary to what one might have expected in a city that readily honors its famous sons and daughters with streets and squares bearing their names, Paris officially ignored

177

his passing. No matter that he was one of France's greatest civil engineers since Vauban, who as *ingénieur du roi* under Louis XIV had scattered his tremendous fortresses throughout the realm. No matter that thirty years had passed since the Panama Affair and Eiffel had in any case been cleared of the miscarriage of justice that had implicated him. The smear on his name remained in certain ultraconservative circles. Finally in 1928 a grateful General Ferrié established a private committee to accept contributions for a token memorial to Eiffel. On May 2, 1929, the simple bust of Eiffel by Antoine Bourdelle, a disciple of Rodin's, was unveiled at the foot of the tower's north pier. On its tall plinth the engraved inscription said only "Eiffel 1832–1923." There were speeches by Ferrié, the director of the Ecole Centrale, an official of the Ministry of Posts and Telegraph and the president of the Paris Municipal Council, who praised "the illustrious engineer who endowed the City of Light with a shining beacon." But not until 1964, on the seventy-fifth anniversary of the tower, did the Council consider the question of naming a Paris street for Eiffel. At last on May 5, 1965, a decree was signed naming a portion of an insignificant street running between the Champs de Mars and the tower Avenue Gustave Eiffel. Avenue Eiffel is only about 100 yards long; its principal traffic is strolling tourists. No houses or buildings front it — there will never be a letter addressed to Avenue Eiffel — and few Parisians know of its existence.

But if Paris' recognition of the man who gave the city its world famous landmark seems too little and too late, it is unfortunately typical of posterity's blinkered view of his achievement. American encyclopedias omit Eiffel's name in their articles on iron railroad bridges and wind tunnels. A comprehensive book tracing the history of engineering from the beginning of civilization to the present contains no index entries between "Egypt" and "Einstein." Apparently thorough volumes on the history of flight completely overlook his work. Eiffel was

178

right to be jealous of the tower, a creation so prodigious, so insistently present, as to blind the world to a remarkably original engineering career that spanned over half a century of the most jarring technical evolution in history.

Still, the fault is not entirely the tower's if its builder has remained relatively obscure. Eiffel's habitual self-effacement made it easy to overlook him as just another pragmatic, sober-sided builder and entrepreneur. Victorian discretion and privacy came naturally to him, and he remained for the most part attractively unimpressed by himself. Eiffel's own explanation of his success was typically modest: "From my father I inherited a taste for adventure, from my mother a love of work and responsibility." Clearly this gifted, sensible Burgundian could have done very nearly anything he set his hand to, and done it well — including the making of fine vinegar.

NINE

AUGUST 25, 1944. In the Eiffel Tower's long, eventful life, marked by all the droll, commercial and often tragic acts that men of fertile imagination could commit, this day must be considered one of the most significant. Standing slender and graceful in the heart of an embattled Paris, the tower seemed to represent everything that the French had longed for during the German occupation. To the war-weary men of General Philippe Leclerc's Second Armored Division it was like a glimpse of the promised land as they speeded their tanks and half-tracks toward the city. Paris' lofty symbol had, after all, survived Hitler's threats to reduce it and the city's other monuments to "a pile of ruins." One tank commander, Captain Georges Buis, later compared sighting the tower to "the Crusaders seeing Jerusalem's walls." And two drivers of half-tracks ended a mad race through Paris beneath the tower's arches — with a dinner at Maxim's to the winner — mindless of whether the structure had been mined by retreating Germans, as many Parisians were convinced. (It had not.) While Allied Shermans and German Panzers jousted in clouds of acrid smoke on the Place de la Concorde, the tower was the site of one of the most

180

evocative vignettes of the Liberation, perhaps the ultimate popular gesture proclaiming the city's freedom.

One man in particular had waited impatiently for this moment, for Lucien Sarniguet, a forty-five-year-old captain in the Paris fire department, had had the duty of lowering the French flag from the tower's mast for the last time on the morning of June 13, 1940. At that time he had vowed to himself to be the first to raise the tricolor when the occupation ended. Now, having eagerly followed, through the clandestine radio broadcasts of the Resistance, the advance of Leclerc's Second Armored, Sarniguet judged that August 25 would be crucial in the battle for Paris and he intended to boost French morale the best way he knew. At noon on that day he arrived at the foot of the Eiffel Tower, accompanied by three men from his detachment carrying a heavy, tattered package tied with a length of laundry rope. In the package was a flag Sarniguet himself had made a few days earlier from old bed sheets and weak wartime dyes of red and blue. He and his men began the ascent of the 1671 steps, despite the battle that raged around the Ecole Militaire, where a German unit was making a determined last stand. When the Germans saw Sarniguet's group climbing the stairs they opened fire on them, sending bullets ricocheting through the tower's iron beams. But what Sarniguet saw above him was worse, in a very personal sense, than the danger from German rifle fire: two other men were already halfway up the stairs with a flag in their arms. He bounded up the steps three at a time but could not catch the others, personnel from the nearby French Naval Museum. Trembling with fatigue and frustration just below the top, Sarniguet watched as the two raised the French flag on the Eiffel Tower for the first time in four years. Then, suddenly forgetting his disappointment, he found himself grinning and hugging the men who had beat him to the top — the occupation was over, as every Parisian knew who saw the tricolor snapping defiantly that afternoon atop their proud tower.

The tower had suffered humiliation along with Paris' citizens during the war. The Germans had quickly seized the Eiffel Tower on June 14, 1940, but not before French radio operators had destroyed its valuable transmission equipment. As a sign of their domination, the Nazis affixed a giant white *V* for victory above the second platform. But they did not dare carry out rumored plans to cut the structure up for scrap in 1942, sensing that the population's reaction would turn toward outright revolt. Occupation troops on leave made the tower a popular tourist attraction once again — 15,000 per day made the ascent during the summer of 1940 — despite their having to walk up. The French Army had ordered the tower's director, Etienne Marc, to destroy completely the elevator systems at the same time the radio equipment was wrecked. But Marc could not bring himself to smash the cabins, pulleys, pumps and the rest. Instead, he cut the cables and put several electric switches and motors out of commission. This did not deter the Germans from installing a radio station at the top, but it was most unfortunate in view of the Führer's visit to Paris the following winter. Hitler, it was said, felt a personal association with the tower — he was born in 1889 — but the nonfunctioning elevators spoiled his tour of it and thwarted his ambition to view Paris, gem of his Thousand Year Reich, spread supine at his feet. He refused to climb the tower's stairs, settling instead for photos of himself taken on the terrace of the Palais de Chaillot with the tower as backdrop.

The occupation authorities forbade anyone but Germans on the tower. The soldiers continued to visit it in droves, paying only a symbolic one-franc admission compared to the prewar price of ten francs. Immediately after the Liberation, American Signal Corps troops climbed up and established their radio post on the third platform, securing communications with the Channel ports, England, and American and French troops operating east and southeast of Paris. (Later, Major General H. C. Ingles, Chief Signal Officer at the War Department, wrote Eiffel's

*Hitler poses before the tower during his visit to Paris:
next best thing to being on it.*

grandson, Robert Salles, to thank him for use of the tower, which had been "of the greatest value to the American and French Forces.") Marc went to work on the elevators as GIs and Parisians began streaming up the stairs in the summer of 1945. Cables and electrical systems had been replaced by June 1 of the following year. Boisterous American troops proved a mixed blessing to the tower. They rendered the service of scratching out the "Fritz, Munich" inscriptions on the tower's wooden handrails and replacing them with the eminently more desirable "Ed, Brooklyn" variety. But the Yanks did show an alarming propensity for tossing empty champagne bottles from the second-platform nightclub. Too happy to dampen the celebrations, the tower's management simply took out special insurance against injury to pedestrians below.

The war over, the tower not only resumed its place as Paris' foremost tourist sight, but also began the steep climb in attendance figures that was to make it one of the most visited monuments in the world. After drawing nearly two million paying visitors during the Exposition of 1889, the tower had declined in popularity until the Exposition of 1900, when a few over one million ascended it. (Having replaced the noisy elevators in the east and west piers with smoother hydraulic units and having strung 5000 electric lights from top to bottom, Eiffel was disappointed in the 1900 figure; but that year the centers of attraction were the Grand Palais and the Petit Palais near the Champs Elysées, a discouragingly long walk from the tower.) Visitors dropped to an all-time low of 121,144 in 1902 and hovered around 200,000 annually until the First World War. The tower was closed to the public from 1915 through 1918, but thereafter it averaged better than half a million tourists until war again closed it in 1940. In 1947 the million mark was passed for the first time since 1900. With postwar prosperity creating world tourism and the tower an obligatory stop on even the most cursory visit to Paris, the figures accelerated steadily:

184

1.5 million in 1956, 2 million in 1963 — the first time the record of 1889 was bettered — 2.5 million in 1969 and 3 million in 1972. To date, nearly seventy million people have visited the tower since its creation. Year in, year out, *la Grande Dame du Champs de Mars* is the most visited monument in France, easily topping the Arc de Triomphe, Notre Dame Cathedral, the châteaux of the Loire Valley and Mont-Saint-Michel. It also outdraws comparable attractions in the United States such as the Washington Monument (two million at best) and the Statue of Liberty (about one million annually). The tower's magnetic appeal prompted one French newspaper columnist to remark that a *touriste* was by definition someone who came to Paris to visit *la Tour*. Three-quarters of the "towerists" are foreign, and of those fully 75 percent are American. When the number of American tourists in Paris dropped in 1973 as a result of the devalued dollar, the Eiffel Tower felt it immediately: admissions dropped several percentage points from those of the previous year.

Those clicking turnstiles at the tower's feet are music to the ears of its owners, the 1600 shareholders of the Société de la Tour Eiffel. The S.T.E. periodically has renewed its lease on the tower from the City of Paris since the first twenty-year lease was granted in 1889. Except for a few years in the doldrums, the tower has been a good business proposition. During its first year of operation all bondholders were reimbursed, and by 1900 the company had distributed $269,280 in dividends. Over the years the S.T.E. has paid a reliable 5 percent dividend, although increasing costs forced the company to suspend payment in 1974 for the first time. Tower shares, which today cost about $20, are widely held by small investors: with 91,800 shares outstanding, only eighty-eight investors own 100 or more. For its current thirty-year lease, which expires at the end of 1979, the company pays the City 18 percent of its gross. The S.T.E. makes a bit on its subrentals — the three restaurants, banquet room, bistro, bar, photography studio and twenty-five souvenir shops — but admissions account for 90 percent of income. With tickets costing sixty cents to the first platform, $1.40 to the second and $2.00 to the top, the 2,914,814 sold in 1973 brought in $3,785,428, up 8 percent from the year before. Surprisingly, over twice as many visitors who leg it up the stairs in the south pier — about 2 percent of total admissions — go on to the second platform as stop on the first. The second platform is also the favorite stop of those who ride up, although during the May to October season when visibility is good the summit has by far the most visitors, up to 4750 per day.

Two full-time supervisory engineers, thirty-seven technicians and eighty other employees operating the elevators, selling tickets and patrolling the platforms keep the tower in running trim. The biggest single maintenance job is painting the tower, or "giving her a new dress" as Parisians inevitably like to put it. Every seven years a contractor brings in a small, agile army of thirty steeplejacks. (Local legend has it that only celibates are accepted for this hazardous job, but that is a bit of harmless Paris folklore; the contractor simply pays a higher insurance premium on his married workers.) They scrub off the accumulated grime, touch up rusty spots with red lead, then lay on one thick coat — fifty-five tons — of a rust-inhibiting silicone and lead paint. Besides possessing special protective qualities, the paint has to be elastic enough not to crack when the tower sways, expands and contracts. All painting must be done by brush, since spray guns would put more paint in the air than on the tower's 15,000 structural members. On a windy day even careful brush work results in complaints from pedestrians, motorists and apartment dwellers in the vicinity of the Champ de Mars who are struck by airborne droplets carried hundreds of yards. To avoid the summer's tourists and winter's rigors, painting can be done only in the spring and fall, so the $300,000, twelve-month job in fact takes two calendar years to complete. The next paint job was to start in 1975.

186

The tower's color has evolved from the original reddish brown to chocolate brown to today's indefinable gray beige, or *ton Tour Eiffel,* as the contractor labels it. The aesthetic technique has remained the same: a darker tone on the lower part of the tower modulating to lighter shades toward the top to accentuate the impression of height. But lively arguments have marked the decision on exactly what color to make the city's symbol. The most recent debate occurred in 1968, when André Malraux as minister of culture lobbied whimsically for a green Eiffel Tower while Maurice Doublet, the prefect of Paris, wanted blue gray, "like the Paris sky." Concerned officials suggested, in all, fifteen colors that year, ranging from a somber dark gray to lively pink and azure blue. *Le Figaro* entered the fray, plumping patriotically for a tricolor tower. S.T.E. officers managed diplomatically to sidestep the wilder ideas, and after everyone had had his fun the company quietly ordered the contractor to go ahead with the discreet gray beige they had wanted all along, feeling this color sets off the tower subtly but effectively against the sky.

Occasionally, Paris thrills to rumors concerning the supposedly parlous condition of the Eiffel Tower. As noted, it was predicted that the tower would fall during its construction. In 1909, the word was that since Eiffel's twenty-year lease was up the tower would be dismantled and moved elsewhere or simply scrapped. While implausible, the idea was not beyond the pale of possibility. Uncertainty over the tower's future after the turn of the century spurred Eiffel to establish more firmly its utilitarian role; his invitation to Ferrié to make use of the tower as a military communications post, for example, was in large part enlightened self-interest. French newspapers find the tower makes good copy, and they delightedly fan the slightest ember of speculation about its imminent demise. Even the solemn *Le Monde* succumbed in 1972 and asked in a scare headline, "Must the Eiffel Tower Be Razed?" The structure was in such

bad condition, the paper reported, that necessary repairs would cost twice the expense of simply tearing it down. Next day presumably anxious Parisians were reassured by the same paper that "The Eiffel Tower Is in Good Health." All the tower needed was partial replacement of its vertical box columns between the second platform and the intermediate platform. Work on the columns actually had begun in 1970 because of corrosion inside them at that level. Below, the columns are large enough to permit a worker to enter them for inspection and painting, but from the second platform up inspection had been impossible and eighty years in Paris' damp climate had taken their toll. Now two sides of each column are being replaced by openwork triangular braces that permit visual checking and painting of the interior. The $680,000 operation was to be completed by 1975.

As part of its continuing maintenance program, the tower is regularly checked via closed-circuit television. While an engineer sits below in the S.T.E. offices near the north pier monitoring a TV screen, workers rove over the tower armed with TV cameras, which they aim systematically at every rivet, truss and beam, enabling the engineer to order repairs and replacements where necessary. Keeping the Grande Dame young is costly: in the two decades from 1950 to 1970, nearly $500,000 was spent annually on maintenance and equipment. But when the twin beacons at the top broke down in 1970, the S.T.E. balked at the $40,000 repair job. Tower officials claimed that France's Civil Aviation Agency had to maintain the beacons as a navigational aid. The Agency denied this responsibility, arguing that the beacons were superfluous to flight safety because planes are forbidden to overfly Paris. Thus have ended the amiable winks from the City of Light that travelers miles away eagerly anticipated when approaching Paris at night. Ordinary, functional, red warning lights, the sort that mark factory chimneys and gas houses, replaced the beacons. Cost accountants may yet squeeze the joie de vivre out of Paris.

189

Left: *Inspecting the tower via
closed-circuit television.*

In terms of illumination, the tower now seems to have hit a low point in brilliance and imagination. To be sure, it is still lighted on occasion by 170 spotlights of 3000 watts each, positioned around it below, but only when other Paris monuments are similarly illuminated on national holidays and at the peak of the tourist season. Most evenings, the tower rides the Paris skyline like a darkened ship running a blockade, visible only at the first and second levels, the dull red lights above scarcely noticeable. Such a lackluster appearance is enough to make one long for the bad old days when the tower served as the biggest illuminated advertising sign ever built.

That occurred in 1925, when André Citroën rented space on the tower to advertise his automobiles. The S.T.E. had been looking for a way to liven up the tower on the occasion of Paris' great Arts Décoratifs exposition that year, which was held nearby. An Italian lighting specialist named Jacopozzi proposed a project on a suitably gigantic scale: the tower would become an immense torch composed of flaming arabesques that turned into stars, shooting comets and animated signs of the zodiac. Tower officials loved the idea but winced at Jacopozzi's price of half a million dollars. Citroën heard of the project and agreed to finance it in return for the right to put his name in lights on the tower in letters ninety-eight feet high along with the company's double chevron symbol. The deal was struck and Jacopozzi went to work. One can only conjecture what Gustave Eiffel would have thought of turning his tower into a luminous billboard outshining even the most outlandish examples of Times Square Art, but he would likely have admired the engineering prowess it entailed. First Jacopozzi installed at the foot of the tower a generating station with a 1200 kilowatt capacity to power his 250,000 lights of six colors. From there he raised a column of thirty-two electrical cables, each as thick as a man's waist, and strung it on a wooden framework which itself weighed 100 tons. The installation required 375 miles of wiring, the whole so carefully camouflaged within the tower's structure

190

Right: *The tower's illumination today.*

as to be virtually invisible. In addition to animated figures and the Citroën name, which ran from the second platform to the top on the three sides facing the center of Paris, pearly strings of lights outlined the tower's arches and lower piers.

The tower went up in its artificial blaze for the first time on July 4, 1925, to the general delight. Each flash of animation lasted five seconds, followed by forty seconds of total illumination and forty more of the Citroën logo. The spectacle was visible twenty-four miles away. Few criticisms of the commercialism of the operation were aired, and in succeeding years it was extended and refined. In 1926 another 125,000 bulbs and 420 miles of wiring were added to create the illusion of cascades of colored water and luminous fountains. In 1927, lightning zigzagged down the tower and it burst into flame, thunderstruck by an additional 4000 bulbs. Commercial or not, the Citroën gimmick was a welcome sight on May 21 of that year to a lone American aviator searching for luminous reference points below as he completed the first trans-Atlantic flight, New York to Paris. Charles Lindbergh later recalled in detail his arrival over the city at 9:52 P.M. and his aerial salute to the tower:

I'm still flying at 4000 feet when I see it, that scarcely perceptible glow, as though the moon had rushed ahead of schedule. Paris is rising over the edge of the earth. It's almost thirty-three hours from my take-off on Long Island. As minutes pass, myriad pin points of light emerge, a patch of starlit earth under a starlit sky — the lamps of Paris — straight lines of lights, curving lines of lights, squares of lights, black spaces in between. Gradually avenues, parks and buildings take outline form; and there, far below, a little offset from the center, is a column of lights pointing upward, changing angles as I fly — the Eiffel Tower. I circle once above it, and turn northeastward toward Le Bourget.

The world's biggest clock, with a face fifty feet in diameter, was the new twist in 1933; the "hands," actually spokes of multicolored lights, operated sequentially to show the hour and

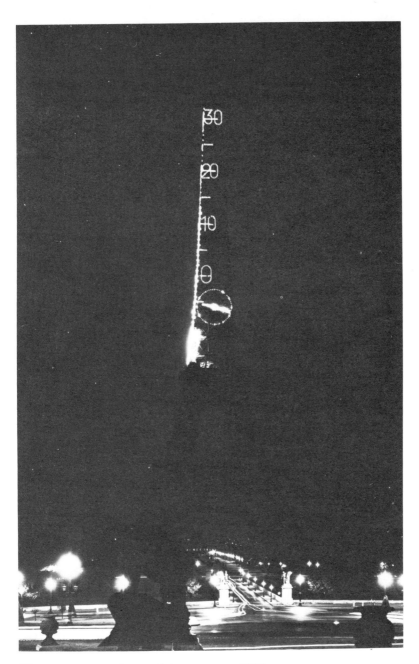

The tower as timepiece and thermometer, 1934.

minute. (This was the second time the tower had been turned into a Brobdingnagian clock; the first was in 1907 when luminous numerals twenty feet high flashed the hour from the second platform.) Jacopozzi's last trick on the tower, in 1934, was to install 1000 more lights and fifteen miles of cables to create a thermometer that reached from the second platform to the top. White lights outlined numerals from zero to thirty degrees centigrade and formed the thermometer's spine. As the temperature rose or fell a parallel line of red lights — the "mercury" — crept up or down; the distance between degrees was eight feet.

Citroën discontinued his sign, which cost approximately $120,000 a year to operate, at the end of 1936. Since then nothing has been created to compare with it and probably never will be, given the more critical cast of public opinion toward such garish promotion gimmicks. Another French automobile maker, Peugeot, wanted to rent space on the tower in 1968 for a much more discreet sign, a luminous "504" and its lion head trademark, to promote a new model. The Paris Municipal Council rejected the project, apparently for aesthetic reasons. The last time the tower really blazed with light was during the Paris world's fair of 1937, when six miles of fluorescent tubes outlined its curving edges and every evening a gigantic display of pyrotechnics shot fountains of fire from the first and second platforms, long colored tracers arching out in all directions. That same year the quaint arcades were removed from the first platform to give the tower a more severely modern appearance. The transformation was unfortunate in the opinion of those who liked the tower with all its quirky originality. But in becoming darker and duller the tower once again faithfully reflected its era: an age of gentle nonsense was fast drawing to a close as the lights, in the statesman's phrase about an earlier period, began going out all over Europe.

Of human nonsense, foolishness and pathos the tower has

195

Left: *Fireworks on the tower at the Paris World's Fair of 1937.*

seen more than its share. Like every unconventional object of significance, it seems to serve as a lightning rod for the race's erratic impulses. Many of the zanier activities associated with the tower have had at least a pretext of serious endeavor, such as Santos-Dumont's dirigible flights and, in 1909, Comte de Lambert's daring flight over the top of it in a flimsy Wright bi-plane. But well before then the tower had begun to attract show-offs and oddballs. In 1891 a Paris baker named Silvain Dornon found brief fame by wobbling up the 363 steps to the first plat-form on a pair of stilts. A Paris sports daily sponsored a foot race up the tower in 1906 which attracted 120 starters. The winner made it to the first platform in three minutes, four sec-onds, a robust lady named Madame Boude finished in eight minutes and a more ambitious contestant charged up the 744 steps to the second platform in the same time with 100 pounds of cement on his shoulders.

In the land of the Tour de France, the bicycle naturally had its place on the tower and in 1923 someone tried a stunt with a *vélo*. In June of that year a Paris sports writer, Pierre Labric, took a turn around the first platform on his bike and then headed for the stairs. He bumped down to the cheers of a band of cronies and rubberneckers in record time — necessarily a rec-ord since he was the first. The world seemed to feel he was wel-come to it, no one challenging it until 1958 when a stunt man from Saint Tropez named Coin-Coin went Labric one better by negotiating the staircase on a unicycle. It is a moot point with tower buffs as to whether Coin-Coin and Labric both were not surpassed by Gilbert Dutrieux, a thirty-nine-year-old Parisian who in 1959 went up the tower instead of down — and did it on one leg rather than one wheel.

Depression and war dampened the imagination of Eiffel Tower nuts, but a few days after the Allies took Paris, it is said, a Flying Fortress of the U.S. Army Air Corps zoomed deftly between the tower's legs. That was the first time a pilot had at-tempted the feat since a twenty-three-year-old Frenchman, Léon

196

Collot, tried it in a light plane in November 1926. Collot's elder brother lived on the Champ de Mars and Léon wanted to give him a thrill by buzzing the tower at grasstop level. He lined up his plane with the Trocadéro, headed in over the Iéna bridge and was doing well until the morning sun, rising behind the École Militaire, caught him square in the eyes. Blinded momentarily, he veered slightly to the left, caught a wing in one of the antenna cables strung from the tower and crashed in flames. Of the hundreds of fatalities associated with the tower, Collot's was the most spectacular.

For the last couple of decades, adventurers — to use the most charitable term — have expressed themselves on the Eiffel Tower by climbing it as if it were an iron mountain. The fad began on a July evening in 1954 when a twenty-two-year-old German student shinnied up through the crossbraces. Around midnight he reached a point above the second platform and settled down on a crossbeam to sleep, waking in time to reach the top by nine the next morning. When he got there he was welcomed by Paris policemen who hustled him to the local *commissariat* for questioning. No charges were pressed and the student, having done his thing, returned to Germany the following day. What had seemed a bit of silliness at the time was consecrated ten years later when it was included in the official celebration of the tower's seventy-fifth anniversary. As part of the festivities in May 1964, four experienced mountain climbers traded their crampons for tennis shoes and charged up the trusswork of the west pier. As Eurovision hookups to fourteen countries allowed some fifty million spectators to follow the action on their television screens, the alpinists clambered by bemused tourists on the first platform, belayed past the overhang at the second platform and followed their Italian leader, Guido Magnone, up the nearly vertical ascent to the crest. At one point it appeared the group might be upstaged by a lone climber in a business suit and street shoes who reached the first platform faster than the professionals. He was a Hungarian house painter who knew the tower well from having helped paint it, but Gyulia Nagy was intercepted by police at the first level and the show went on. After the four reached the top, Magnone made a crowd-pleasing rappel straight down through the center of the tower, riding a rope in a harness with a brake to control his speed. His companions, their work finished for the day, took the elevators down.

Except for a Norman cow named Kilkee that was hoisted up in 1968 to promote dairy products, most of the more lighthearted attacks on the Eiffel Tower's dignity lately have had a sporting angle of some sort. Others have scaled Mount Eiffel, at least part way. Usually they are caught by Paris' long-suffering *flics* before reaching the top, although a particularly well-organized group of five French students did succeed in making it all the way up in January 1972. In 1969 there was a project to erect an artificial ski slope of plastic from the first platform to the ground. City-bound Parisians would then be able to slalom down the 600-foot slope on winter days and end up in a simulacrum of an Alpine village complete with chalets and skating rink. Alas, the Eiffel Slope never got off the ground for lack of financing. The tower also served as locus for Paris' first view of streaking, a minor sport that flourished in the spring of 1974, when thirteen Americans in the first flower of manhood dashed nude beneath its arches.

On the whole, though, it is not the lighter but the darker side of an unbalanced human psyche that responds most often to the tower. On an August evening two years after it was built, a demented printer's mechanic gravely climbed fifty feet up the north pier, lighting his way with the butts of three candles. He undressed, left a note willing his clothes to Gustave Eiffel and carefully hanged himself. His was the first of the 360-odd suicides to date on the Eiffel Tower: one every three months, on average, since 1889.* The tower cannot claim a world's record in

* No official count of suicides on the tower has ever been kept; this is the figure generally used by Paris newspapers, based on an unofficial tally.

this grim field — the Golden Gate Bridge, located in the city with the highest suicide rate in the United States, has been the jumping-off place for nearly 500 suicides since its construction in 1937 — but more despondents have chosen it for their last act than any other place in Paris, including the bridges on the Seine. Only about twenty known suicides have been committed, for example, from the towers of Notre Dame.

Perhaps the *douceur de vivre* of the Belle Epoque precluded such ghastly gestures. Whatever the reason, no one leaped to his death from the Eiffel Tower until 1911, after it had been a fixture in Paris for twenty-two years. Even then, the leap was on the pretext of a scientific experiment. A tailor named Teichelt from the Paris suburb of Longjumeau had made a spring-loaded bat-wing cape which, he contended, would enable him to fly. Perhaps having heard that earlier in the year an inventor named Hervieu had successfully jumped from the first platform to test a parachute for aviators, Teichelt requested permission from the S.T.E. to do the same with his cape. With considerable trepidation, the company acceded to his request on condition that he also obtain police authorization and sign a waiver clearing the company of any responsibility in the event of accident. He complied and showed up with a handful of well-wishers at 8 o'clock on an exceptionally cold December morning. Press photographers were on hand as well. Once on the ledge of the first platform, Teichelt's courage faltered, but goaded by taunts from excited spectators and blasé photographers he finally stepped timidly over the edge. His complicated cape fluttering uselessly, the poor man assumed the aerodynamic characteristics of a rock. The hole he dug in the frosty earth beneath the tower was nearly a foot deep.

The grisly precedent had been set. Barely eight months later a young woman rode up to the third platform, calmly mounted a stool to reach the narrow, chest-high observation window, squeezed through and landed in pieces on the second platform. She literally had been cut in two when she struck a crossbeam on

199

the way down. Since then the Eiffel Tower has witnessed the despair of a cross-section of humanity: from a schoolboy of fifteen depressed by bad marks to a young actress who felt she had failed in the theater to a wealthy playboy to a man of seventy-five with an incurable disease — the tower has been both their way out of an unendurable impasse and a final, dramatic refusal of anonymity. Most suicides have been French, but many have been foreign, some coming to Paris for the express purpose of jumping from the tower. Periodically there were public outcries for antisuicide measures, but the S.T.E. was reluctant to put up extra-high guard rails for fear of impairing the view and giving the tower a sinister, besieged appearance. Besides, it was argued, if a person cannot commit suicide on the Eiffel Tower he will simply choose the Seine or another of the many methods available. There was the reported case of a middle-aged man who had hopped over the railing of the first platform and at the last minute was prevented from falling by a tower guard who caught his leg. Hauled back, he was taken to the restaurant and given a free lunch to cheer him up. He admitted he could think of no valid reason to commit suicide, and, apparently fully recovered from his fit of depression, he happily offered to buy champagne for his hosts. To insure that the man made it home all right, a tower employee drove him to his house in the suburbs. The next morning he was found drowned, lying face down in one of the small duck ponds near the foot of the tower. Apparently he had returned to the tower that night, found it locked and decided to die as near it as possible. He was only one of several such incorrigibles who subsequently killed themselves after being saved on the tower.

On the other hand, increased prevention obviously could save lives. As an example of how little is sometimes necessary, the story is told of a man who had come to the tower with the intention of committing suicide but had changed his mind when he missed the elevator. He decided not to wait for the next one, went home and wrote a letter to the S.T.E. telling of the incident and enclosing fifty francs for the elevator operator who had unwittingly saved his life. There were other happy endings. In March 1963 a young woman jumped from the first platform but became entangled in the trusswork and was retrieved, unharmed, by firemen; the following August she gave birth to a healthy baby boy. In 1964 a woman who leaped from the first level landed on the compliant roof of a Renault Dauphine and escaped with only a ruptured spleen.

But 1964 saw the worst acceleration of suicides in the history of the tower. Fatal leaps were averaging one per month, sometimes occurring within twenty-four hours of each other as sensational press coverage tended to encourage a snowball effect. Number 335 on September 7 was a woman of forty-one. Number 336, the next day, was a man of thirty-three, who managed to shake loose when a guard attempted to hold him back by his coattails. Number 337, a month later, was a woman of fifty who jumped from the second platform, bounced twice on the west pier and crashed through the awning of the first platform restaurant. At this point two Paris municipal councilors sent an urgent demand to the Paris prefect to find a way to stop the slaughter. Prefect Haas-Picard appointed a study commission that proposed three possible solutions: a large open grille around each platform, plate-glass barriers above the existing handrails or nets beneath each platform to catch jumpers. These measures were initially rejected by the prefect because, as he said, "All three would be ugly or ineffective or dangerous for the stability of the tower due to greater wind resistance. Besides, if people cannot jump from the platforms they can still jump from the stairs, and we can't put a guard on every step."

But public pressure increased as the bodies continued to rain down, and murder on the tower was added to its already catastrophic suicide record when a Spaniard pushed his wife from the second platform while pretending to attempt to hold her back. For a while the top area was blocked off as a preventive measure — and the first day it was closed a sixty-year-old man was

201

stopped by a guard on the second platform as he swung a leg over the edge. Finally in early 1965 Haas-Picard ordered the S.T.E. to put up a five-and-one-half-foot steel wire fence around each platform. The wires were eight inches apart to permit tourists to poke their cameras through for snapshots of Paris. But determined suicides easily managed to scale the fences. Nine months and twelve deaths later, the S.T.E. heightened the barriers to ten feet, with a backward overhang on the second level to make it still more difficult to get over. The observation platform at the top was completely caged in. Today two or three persons per year continue to evade patrolling guards, negotiate the barrier and leap to their deaths.

Besides involuntarily becoming a notorious suicide spot, the tower has had other troubles. First it was announced that the structure would be moved a few yards so as to span the Seine — two feet on the Left Bank and two on the Right — with the Iéna bridge running beneath. Sometime later came the news that the tower was to be loaned to Greece as a goodwill gesture. The plan was to dismantle it and place the pieces in hatboxes specially designed by a Paris couturier. As it happened, both announcements occurred on the first of April of different years and both were April Fools' jokes perpetrated respectively by the French television network and a Paris newspaper.

But the fire that destroyed the television relay station and weather bureau facilities atop the tower the night of January 3, 1956, was real enough. When firemen arrived they found that only a few gallons of water were available for their hoses, and watched helplessly as intense heat destroyed eighty tons of equipment and popped rivets in the iron beams of the third platform. The entire supporting structure at the top was deformed and had to be rebuilt at a cost of $100,000 while approximately half of Paris went for several months without its ration of TV programs. Fortunately the wooden walls of Gustave Eiffel's private studio, which has been preserved as he left it, had been replaced by iron the month before, saving it from destruction.

202

No sooner had repairs been completed than the tower suffered the indignity of having its flagpole removed for good in favor of a new TV antenna. The tower gained sixty-six feet in the process, becoming 1052 feet four inches tall, but many Parisians were inconsolable over losing it as the city's flagstaff. Even those who were never reconciled to the existence of the thing found its justification in its role as magnificent bearer of the tricolor. Indeed, not since the day Lucien Sarniguet lost the race with his homemade ensign had the tower played that role so fully as in April 1957 during the official visit of Queen Elizabeth II to Paris. On that occasion two French and two British flags, each sixteen by thirty-nine feet, flew in full pomp from the tower's mast. But two months later the antenna went up and the mast came down. "Paris will forever miss its ultimate embellishment," lamented one columnist.

The Eiffel Tower may not have been sold as many times as the Brooklyn Bridge, but a number of confidence men have nonetheless managed to make money out of it. The story goes that the first was a sharper from Prussian Silesia who claimed in 1891 to have a contract to make a sheath that would protect the tower in winter. He found a businessman in Brandenburg willing to put up the funds to purchase miles of canvas — and was never heard from again. Since that time the tower's name has been taken in vain to promote several swindles, often involving recuperation of those 7000 tons of iron or painting the tower with special antirust products. One of those recurrent stories in Paris papers about the need to tear down the tower prompted such a con in 1925. Count Victor Lustig (among his twenty-three other aliases) and his associate, "Dapper Dan" Collins, were operating in Paris at the time and noticed the article. Lustig contacted five salvage companies, introduced himself as an official from the city office with jurisdiction over the Eiffel Tower and invited them to bid for the demolition job. He rented an imposing suite in the Hôtel de Crillon for the occasion, explaining to the firms' representatives that the ultrasecret negotiations could not be held in his office because of the need for maximum discretion. Lustig took the highest bid, amounting to several million francs, and then coolly accepted in addition a bribe from his mark before catching the Orient Express for Vienna. The victim was too embarrassed to complain to the police, and Lustig and Collins "sold" the tower a second time before heading for America and a series of highly profitable jobs there. Lustig was finally convicted of counterfeiting in 1935 and sent to Alcatraz.

Modern day protesters have used the tower as the means to their diverse ends, political or otherwise. A group of Cubans hung a twenty-foot black and red flag from the first platform in March 1958 to promote Fidel Castro's revolutionary 26 of July movement and decry the sixth anniversary of Batista's coup d'état. The tower was again the medium of protest during Vice President Hubert Humphrey's tumultuous official visit to Paris in April 1967, when demonstrators against the Vietnam War strung a giant "U.S. Go Home" banner on it. And one irate citizen chose the tower in January 1968 as the ideal spot from which to protest what he considered the poor quality of French television programs: he hauled his TV set up to the first platform and threw it off.

The tower's closest call came during France's Algerian War. Terrorists of the National Liberation Front had already exploded bombs in many parts of Paris when they decided to hit the tower in order to knock out of commission the television and radio equipment — including transmitters of the police and gendarmerie. On September 23, 1958, shortly after Charles de Gaulle came to power, N.L.F. terrorists planted a five-pound charge of dynamite, attached to a clockwork timer, in the ladies' rest room on the third platform. The bomb was found the next morning by a cleaning lady, appropriately named Madame Angèle, who alerted the tower's guards and Armand Triffoz, an engineer. Triffoz grabbed the bomb and carried it outside so it would cause less damage if it exploded. The police bomb squad arrived and defused the device, which had malfunctioned; they said later that had the bomb gone off it would have blown away the entire top of the tower. For his heroism Triffoz was awarded the Silver Medal of the City of Paris, presented by René Le Grain-Eiffel. Four years later, as the Algerian War drew to a close with the N.L.F. victorious, it was France's extreme rightist Secret Army Organization that was throwing bombs in Paris to protest at De Gaulle's policy of independence for Algeria. When the S.A.O. terrorist code-named Castille was arrested, police found complete plans for dynamiting the tower's north pier. With that leg gone, the structure would have collapsed into the Seine.

Seemingly impervious to everything men have tried, from the Belle Epoque to the Age of Anxiety, the Grande Dame serenely continues to tick off her milestones. Usually some simple rites mark the passage of the years, as when, in 1939, the Duke and Duchess of Windsor presided over a beauty contest to celebrate the tower's fiftieth anniversary — girls had to be over six feet tall to compete for the title of Miss Eiffel Tower — and Mass was said on the first level. The S.T.E. presented automobiles to the twenty-five millionth visitor in 1953 and the thirty-five millionth in 1959. (The latter was an eleven-year-old country lad visiting the capital who said he would turn the car over to *maman* because all he ever expected to drive was a tractor.) That year coincided with the tower's seventieth anniversary, and to fête the occasion 135 Parisians born in 1889 were invited to a gala luncheon at the second platform restaurant. In 1964 the Archbishop of Paris, Cardinal Feltin, celebrated High Mass on the tower to mark the seventy-fifth anniversary. Besides the Mass and the scaling of the tower by mountain climbers, the structure was festooned with a neon tricolor and the figures 1889 and 1964. The eighty-fifth anniversary, on the other hand, passed in obscurity; 1974 was a tight year for the S.T.E. because of rising costs, despite continued high admission figures. As reflected in the tower, contemporary prosperity appears increasingly fragile in the face of inflation. Meanwhile the Eiffel Tower goes on exercising its quasi-

205

mystical appeal to the masses, who respond not only with yearly pilgrimages by the millions but with a constant flow of mail. A random sampling of the dozens of letters received annually by the S.T.E. reveals the range of curiosity and interest the tower sparks in a wide spectrum of humanity. A Turkish engineer wants to know the exact mathematical formula of the tower's curving columns, for example, and a high school student in Kansas asks how many tons of paint are required to cover it. The tower received a flowery birthday card on its eighty-third anniversary from a schoolgirl in Bremen, and one of her countrymen in the Eifel region wonders who built the Eiffel Tower and "Why do you spell it with two *f*'s?" The Performing Arts Abroad group in Kalamazoo, Michigan, offers to give a concert on the first platform. A lady restaurateur in California asks the secret of the warmer in the tower's snack bar that heats hot dog buns from the inside. The story published by *Le Monde* questioning the tower's health was picked up by international news agencies, prompting a spate of concerned letters from around the world asking whether it was true that the tower would have to be torn down. One engineering firm in Bangkok saw a business opportunity in the allegedly tottering tower and offered to rebuild it, noting that it had already restored Bangkok's Temple of Dawn.

And then there is a young lady in Vermont who asks, "Why do all the people come to the tower? What has the tower got inside?" Her naive questions are the same as those that many have attempted to answer over the years in one way or another. For implicit in the foolishness and drama that have attended it during its history is the unexpected significance that man's tallest tower has assumed. Created to proclaim the preening pride of the nineteenth century, the tower has become an object of fascination and obsession, a touchstone and totem of surprising evocative power, as twentieth-century artists, poets and philosophers were to discover.

206

TEN

WHEN GUSTAVE EIFFEL DIED in 1923 his tower was still the tallest manmade edifice of any sort in the world. It would remain so until 1929 — a reign of exactly forty years — when the 1046-foot Chrysler Building was completed in New York, followed by the 1250-foot Empire State Building two years later. Since then, utilitarian structures over a thousand feet tall have become commonplace. In the last twenty years television masts have proliferated across the globe from one in Tokyo frankly modeled on the Eiffel Tower and standing 1092 feet high, to a 1750-footer of reinforced concrete in Moscow, to the tallest yet: a guyed antenna near Fargo, North Dakota, 2063 feet high, equivalent to the Eiffel Tower, Washington Monument and Great Pyramid together. Modern construction techniques permit prosaic factory chimneys to reach over a quarter of a mile high. With tall constructions sprouting like mushrooms after a spring shower, it is hazardous to label any the tallest, but the Canadian National Railroad claims that its tower in Toronto is the tallest freestanding structure — 1805 feet, including a 300-foot communications mast at its top.

Towers are rivaled in height by high-rise apartment and office

*Paris skyscrapers encroach upon a skyline once dominated
solely by the Eiffel Tower.*

buildings, pushed ever higher by metropolitan land costs. No
sooner are the 110-story twin towers of the World Trade Center
in New York declared the tallest buildings in the world at 1350
feet than the Sears Tower in Chicago reaches 1800 feet with the
help of 350-foot TV antennas. Architects today consider 3000-
foot skyscrapers feasible. Even Paris, where the Eiffel Tower
provoked such heated protests less than a century ago, is now
ringed about with unimaginative tall buildings possessing all the
aesthetic appeal of shoeboxes stood on end and none of the
tower's doughty originality. Parisians complain halfheartedly
about them — particularly the hideous, 690-foot Tour Maine-
Montparnasse, the tallest building in Europe, which dominates
the city like some dark, money-swollen Moloch — but the days
are long past when they cared enough about the beauty of their
city to risk appearing quixotic in combating such eyesores.

208

And yet despite the frenzied construction of television antennas and multistory buildings, the Eiffel Tower is still the tallest *tower*. Every taller structure built since has had some specific commercial or useful purpose, either as a communications tool or shelter. Not since France's Exposition of 1889 has anyone thrown up so high a tower *qua* tower, a ladder to the sky with no other fundamental purpose than allowing man to climb up and have a look around. Never again was the persistent impulse so great to express a people's aspiration and accomplishment through erection of a gratuitously tall structure. The British, to be sure, wanted to better the French as soon as the Eiffel Tower was up. Hardly had the Paris Exposition closed than Benjamin Baker, celebrated builder of the Forth Bridge, opened a contest for designs of a tower 1200 feet tall. Seventy projects were submitted and two were awarded prizes, although the jury admitted that "The existence of the Eiffel Tower and desire to avoid imitating it considerably increase the difficulty of the problem, for it represents the most rational use of architectural and economic means." Work on the iron tower began in June 1893 in Wembley Park, near London. Seven months later the structure had reached the level of the Eiffel Tower's first platform, but the project gave out at that point. London had to wait nearly a century for its tall tower, the ungainly and thoroughly utilitarian Post Office Tower, at 620 feet not quite two-thirds as high as the Eiffel Tower.

The impulse continues to exercise men's imaginations, but designers keep bumping up against the problem confronting Benjamin Baker: the Eiffel Tower is inimitable. For the World's Fair of 1932, Chicago wanted to build a 2060-foot steel tower that would accommodate 4000 people on its observation platform, but the $3 million project never came off. Saint Louis' steel Gateway Arch, completed in 1965 at a cost of $29 million, gets around the difficulty of imitating the Eiffel Tower by being a parabolic curve, but it rises "only" 630 feet. In Paris itself an artist named Nicholas Schoffer advanced a harebrained scheme

209

The Eiffel Tower compared to the tallest structures in the world at the time of its construction.

in 1972 for a "cybernetic light tower" 1300 feet tall to be constructed among the high-rise office buildings in the suburb of La Défense. A rectangular metal cage, the tower was to be equipped with multicolored, electronically programmed flashing lights and revolving mirrors to create random patterns in the Paris sky. It was also to cost $40 million, a figure that, if nothing else did it, apparently deterred Paris authorities from authorizing what surely would have been the city's ultimate visual nightmare.

Other present day builders of towers simply pattern their designs on the Eiffel Tower — or dream of importing it whole. A 340-foot replica of the tower was built in King's Mill, Ohio, as part of an amusement park in 1972. Miami entertains the idea of constructing a thousand-foot tower for its Inter-American Center in conjunction with the United States Bicentennial in 1976; officers of the construction firm studying the project visited the Eiffel Tower in September 1972 and talked with S.T.E. engineers for information on how Eiffel did it. Montreal wanted a tall tower for its Expo 67 and first considered transporting the Eiffel Tower to the Ile Sainte Hélène. When this was shown to be impracticable, the fair's organizers had plans drawn up for a structure taller than the Eiffel Tower and invited the City of Paris to help finance it. Paris declined, and Montreal abandoned the project. Another attempt to import the tower was made by a real estate man in North Myrtle Beach, South Carolina, in 1974, after he was told by a guide during a visit to Paris that the Eiffel Tower was for sale. He decided that it was just the thing his town needed. With support from city officials he applied to the Federal Aviation Agency for permission to put a thousand-foot tower in the area of the local airport. After all, he explained to a reporter, "They took the London Bridge and moved it over here brick by brick." The S.T.E. said that as it happened the tower was not for sale.

Images of the tower in every conceivable form have been popular since the Exposition of 1889. Indeed, the question of souvenirs got Gustave Eiffel into a lawsuit early in the tower's first year of existence, for he had granted exclusive rights to the Printemps department store to make and sell tower trinkets. He had reckoned without the power of France's artisans and small shopkeepers, who won a class-action suit against him for the right to part of the business. Since then the variety of objects for sale bearing the tower's likeness has multiplied beyond the fondest dreams of French *schlockmeisters*. The items number several hundred, including the numerous versions of miniature towers from the size of a bracelet charm to a table lamp, some with colored lights inside, others bearing thermometers or enclosed in a glass ball filled with imitation snow. Then there are the everyday objects struck with the tower in some form, including cuff links, ladies' compacts, atomizers, table flatware, penknives, scissors, paperweights, cane heads, umbrella handles, cigar cutters, cigarette holders, pipes, scarves, brooches — the inventory goes on and on. It is said that the only visitor who ever bought one of every item on sale was Emperor Hirohito. Surveys of Paris department stores reveal that the tower comes first in the hearts of American souvenir hunters but that the history-minded British prefer busts of Napoleon.

The pervasive desire for a replica or relic of the Eiffel Tower goes beyond mere souvenirs and takes on the dimension of fetishism. The number of model Eiffel Towers lovingly made by individuals under its benign charm is unknown, but several have come to light over the years, cases amazing for the hours spent in painstaking thoroughness. In the 1930s a dental student in New York built a ceiling-high scale model Eiffel Tower, appropriately enough of 11,000 toothpicks. In 1963 a five-foot model was made in Buenos Aires, also of toothpicks but with a difference — they came from fifty-seven countries. In France a watchmaker named Georges Vitel mobilized his wife and son every weekend and holiday for several years to put together a model incorporating two and a half million matchsticks and 2000 feet of electrical wiring. Eight thousand hours of work by the trio produced a one-tenth scale model of fanatical detail down to working elevators, electric lights, tables and chairs in the tower's restaurants and a bed in Gustave Eiffel's third platform apartment. American cultists include an Ohioan who in 1972 wrote the S.T.E. for the tower's exact dimensions, then built a seven-foot model of 704 handcut pieces of perforated aluminum. About the same time, Howard Porter of Detroit wrote for data and then spent 300 hours on a 1/250 scale model using 110 fireplace matches, 1080 ordinary kitchen matches and 1200 toothpicks, which he assembled with half a pound of glue and a pair of locking dental tweezers. Porter kept the S.T.E. informed of his progress with letters and photographs and climaxed his labors with a trip to Paris for his first view of the real tower and lunch on the second platform with S.T.E. officials.

With passing time the Eiffel Tower appears to assume an increasing status as talisman of the modern world. It was invoked, for instance, at the New York World's Fair of 1964–1965 as a sort of patron saint of progress. When construction of the fair's symbol, the stainless steel Unisphere, began with a ceremony in Flushing Meadow on March 6, 1963, René Le Grain-Eiffel and Baron Alexis de Gunzburg, then president of the S.T.E., were invited to attend. One hundred forty feet high and weighing 40,000 pounds, Unisphere was seen by the fair's organizers and its makers, the U.S. Steel Corporation, as a continuation of the Eiffel Tower idea. The president of U.S. Steel, Roger Blough, said at the ceremony:

> This tower was the product of the genius and the daring of one of the great builders, Alexandre Gustave Eiffel, who also pioneered the use of the materials of his day in structurally designed concepts for bridges, buildings and viaducts, even before his imagination and courage produced the great tower of which

213

we speak. It is most appropriate that as we begin the construction of Unisphere, we pause in tribute to a man whose technical achievements have inspired so much progress in building and in design.

Mr. Blough then presented to Gustave Eiffel's grandson a stainless steel plaque engraved with juxtaposed drawings of the Eiffel Tower and Unisphere and the text:

Man's achievement in an expanding universe. Eiffel Tower, 1889, Unisphere, 1964. Commemorating start of construction of Unisphere. The theme symbol of the New York World's Fair, 1964–1965, and honoring Gustave Eiffel, magician in iron, engineer, designer, master builder, innovator and creator of Eiffel Tower, symbol of the 1889 Paris International Exposition.

Later, when the 100-story John Hancock Center in Chicago was topped out on May 6, 1968, the insurance firm placed a memento of the Eiffel Tower atop the 1107-foot skyscraper's steel framework. At a ceremony held exactly seventy-nine years after the opening of the tower, the company affixed a time capsule, whimsically called a Skystone, to the roof of the building, which was then the second tallest in the world after the Empire State. Into the capsule went an original letter signed by John Hancock, a fragment of wood from the Hancock House in Boston, historical books and documents — and a triangular wedge of iron from the Eiffel Tower flown over aboard an Air France jet, rather like including a bit of the True Cross in a reliquary.

Even Paris has officially reconciled itself to the tower, albeit long after the structure had been wholeheartedly accepted by Parisians and become the city's de facto totem. On the occasion of Gustave Eiffel's death, the tower was eulogized nearly as much as its creator; one mass circulation daily stated that "all in all, this audacious construction is a veritable chef d'oeuvre of French art." Masterpiece or not, the tower became even more ubiquitous and unavoidable than Maupassant could have imagined in his worst fits of depression over it. Since the early days of the century, no map or other schema of Paris, scarcely a travel poster or advertisement associated with France has appeared without an image of the tower to create immediate identification. When managers of the country's largest newspaper, *France-Soir*, wanted to state visually the equivalent of the ad, "In Philadelphia, nearly everybody reads the *Bulletin*," they put up posters showing an Eiffel Tower in a sitting position reading their paper. And when a big French bank, Crédit Lyonnais, wanted to advertise the opening of a branch in New York, its full-page ads in American magazines showed not a bank but an Eiffel Tower superimposed over the buildings of lower Manhattan.

Not until 1964 did the French government finally recognize the tower as an important part of the country's heritage. André Malraux declared the structure a historical monument, insuring that it may not be altered in any way without special authorization. Roland Barthes, the noted French philosopher, observes that "The surprising thing is that Paris waited so long to acquire its symbol. The Eiffel Tower became Paris through metonymy." Another writer, Philippe Barrès, holds that the tower is as important a part of Paris' mystique as any other monument in this city of symbols:

> Notre Dame represents the Faith, the Institute and University are the life of the mind, the Panthéon is service rendered the nation, the Elysée Palace symbolizes the State, the Louvre art and history, the Arc de Triomphe and the Invalides mean glory. Even the Eiffel Tower, so often criticized, has its meaning for us. At the turn of the century it symbolized the vitality of our know-how which keeps us at the forefront of modern competition.

The Eiffel Tower did not have to wait for official recognition to become a subject for poets, painters and pundits. Hardly had the mini-tempest of the artists' protest died down when Paris songwriters began turning out ditties about the tower for the edification of crowds along the Belle Epoque's boulevards. One popular song of the period called "At 300 Meters Up" begins, "What vertigo it gives you!/Paris so grandiose doesn't look like much/At 300 meters up," and goes on to recount the adventures of pretty, complaisant ladies under the tower's spell on the third platform, the peccadillos of stereotyped English tourists and the like. Another song saw everyone profiting from the tower, including café owners, taxi drivers and so on, but with cobblers making the biggest windfall profits of all, "Because the tower is nine hundred feet." Still another described an Eiffel Tower raising its head high in the sky, mocking Garnier, Dumas and Meissonier and gaily challenging passing clouds, "Halt or I'll cut you in two!" Probably the best-known of all, popularized by Maurice Chevalier and Patachou to the point of becoming the Eiffel Tower's theme song, goes:

> Paris, mais c'est la tour Eiffel
> Avec sa pointe qui monte au ciel.
> Qu'on la trouve laide, qu'on la trouve belle,
> Y'a pas d'Paris sans tour Eiffel.
> On la débine, on la charrie,
> Pourtant, partout ce n'est qu'un cri:
> Paris n's'rait pas Paris sans elle,
> Paris, mais c'est la tour Eiffel!

During the First World War a poem praised the tower's role as communications center for the French Army: "We know that by night you give the orders for the battle,/That by day you guide it. And we think you are beautiful/Both fortress and lace." And during the depressing days of Nazi occupation Mistinguette cheered Parisians nightly by singing "The Eiffel Tower Is Still There" in her review at the Casino de Paris.

The tower began to win its place in literature in the 1920s with Jean Cocteau's ballet-play, *Les Mariés de la Tour Eiffel*, in

216

which it served as backdrop for a gentle satire of La Belle Epoque, complete with a clownish army general who ran around the stage crying "Let's eat! Let's eat!" But Cocteau treated the tower gallantly as "Notre Dame of the Left Bank . . . the queen of Paris." In a later work he called the tower affectionately "a cage of bluebirds." Suddenly the tower became a legitimate subject for French poets. Guillaume Apollinaire called it "The shepherdess of the clouds," and expanding his metaphor, began one poem, "Shepherdess, O Eiffel Tower, your flock of bridges is bleating this morning." During the war Apollinaire thumbed his nose at the Nazis with a saucy poem innocuously entitled "The Eiffel Tower," which by graphic legerdemain managed to insult the occupiers without their knowing it. The letters of the poem were composed to form the outline of the tower, making them difficult to read by anyone whose French was shaky. But the message easily got through to Apollinaire's public: "Hello world, of which I am the eloquent tongue which your mouth, O Paris, will forever stick out at the Germans."

"The staircase to infinity" was what Léon-Paul Fargue grandly termed the tower on one occasion. On another he called it "The *i* of Paris firing its dot like a glorious cannon towards the beauty of interstellar space." And the poet admitted to peculiar visions: "I can hear the Eiffel Tower falling down. Its dinosaur's tail ends at Brest or Toulon. And along with my forty million countrymen I am buried in broken lamps and shreds of sky. In the morning the proud giraffe has grown a hundred yards taller." Jean Giraudoux was probably the writer most impressed by the tower, judging by his published reactions to it. He first of all found it an excellent vantage point from which to admire his favorite city, "the thousand acres of world where most has been thought, spoken and written. The planet's hub, the most free, the most elegant, the least hypocritical." "Mon Dieu," he exclaimed in "My Pretty Eiffel Tower," "what confidence its engineer possessed in universal gravity! Holy Virgin, if the law of gravity had been contradicted for only a quarter of a second, what a magnificent catastrophe it would have been! But this is what can be created with hypotheses. Here, realized in iron, is the rope thrown to the sky by the fakir and which he invites his friends to climb. Mon Dieu, how beautiful it is . . ."

But poets were tardy in discovering the Eiffel Tower compared to painters, who immediately saw its visual potency and savored, as one aesthete put it, Eiffel's "purely dynamic conception of space." As early as 1889 Seurat did a magnificent pointillist canvas full of shimmering parti-colored light as though the tower were seen through a luminous mist. At the same time another impressionist, Louis Hayet, a protegé of Pissarro's, saw the tower in the Paris cityscape as the natural counterpoint to the obelisk in the Place de la Concorde — still one of the best places from which to view the tower. Aesthetically the Eiffel Tower had much in common with modern art, being, like modern paintings and sculptures, an end in itself, its own subject.

For the next fifty years the tower figured in works by Pissarro, Chagall, Gromaire, Dufy, Henri Rousseau, Picasso, Utrillo and Van Dongen among others, representing the impressionist, fauve, cubist and futurist schools and their offshoots. For them the tower was literally the inevitable subject, one they could not get away from, one whose mathematical definition of space drew them like moths to a flame. Of them all, the most fascinated was Robert Delaunay, whose cubistic vision dissected the structure from every possible point of view in an important series of paintings done from 1909 to 1911. Influenced initially by Cézanne and Seurat, Delaunay was on his way to becoming one of the precursors of nonfigurative painting, breaking down a subject into prisms of color; his work had impact on the German Blue Riders such as Paul Klee, and eventually inspired a related style among American painters like S. Macdonald-Wright and Morgan Russell which was the first move in the United States toward abstract art. The French poet Blaise Cendrars was a close companion of

218

The tower as seen by Robert Delaunay, 1910.

Delaunay's during those years and described the artist's dilemma in portraying the tower:

> In 1911 Delaunay did, I believe, fifty-one canvases of the Eiffel Tower before getting the desired result. No artistic formula known could resolve plastically the case of the tower. Realism diminished the impression of height; the ancient laws of Italian perspective made it look skinny. When we viewed it from a distance it dominated Paris, stiff and perpendicular; when we approached it, it seemed to bend and lean over us. Seen from the first platform it twisted, and seen from the top it appeared to fold in upon itself, legs spread and neck pulled in. Delaunay wanted not only to show the tower, but to situate it in Paris.
>
> Finally he took the tower apart in order to place it in its natural framework. He truncated it and inclined it to give the impression of vertigo it inspires; he adopted ten different viewpoints, fifteen perspectives so that part of it is seen from below, part from above, while the buildings around it are shown from left and right, from above and below . . .

Having been painted by artists from every imaginable angle, it was only fitting that the tower serve as art gallery, a role it fulfilled in 1955 when an exhibit of Utrillo's paintings of Paris scenes was held on the first platform. The critics were enchanted at being able to compare Utrillo's personal vision with reality, as one wrote, "from the only place in Paris where the whole city is visible."

The tower has also inspired film makers. Many films have been shot using it as setting or theme, perhaps the most memorable being the ineffable *Lavender Hill Mob*, in which Alec Guiness is involved in a plot to transport gold stolen from the Bank of England in the form of miniature Eiffel Towers, and which ends in a chase scene through the tower's girders. In France, René Clair has been the *cinéaste* most fascinated by the tower. He began his film-making career in 1924 with a work of science fiction, *Paris Qui Dort,* in which a mad scientist anesthetized the population of

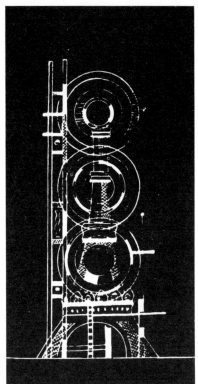

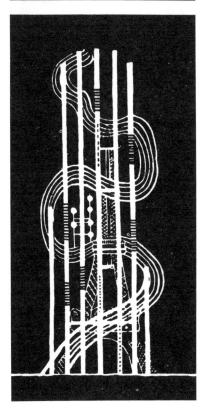

*Three playful projects by Fernand
Léger for illuminating the tower.*

Paris except for a handful of persons who happened to be on the tower's third platform. Then Clair, who liked to say, "The Eiffel Tower is the church steeple of my village," returned to the tower in 1928 to do a lyrical documentary devoted entirely to it and called simply *La Tour*. He treated the tower as an abstraction, using a few special effects such as making the elevators approach each other on the same track and then fuse and disappear, but mainly concentrating on impressions of webbing and tracery produced by girders and trusswork. The result is a masterful study of the Eiffel Tower as archetype, conveying a compelling feeling of mechanical intricacy and vertiginous height.

Examining the Eiffel Tower rather later than artists and poets, some intellectuals have discovered in it a rich mine of metaphor and meaning. Its historical significance has been pointed out by several, though seldom in the sweeping terms of one sociologist, Joseph Foliet, who sees the tower as the most apt label for our era, declaring that "European civilization, after having been Roman, Carolingian, Gothic, Rennaissance and Baroque, has become in the 20th century the Civilization of the Eiffel Tower."

Roland Barthes, who probably has done more high-flown philosophizing about the tower than any other thinker, finds that the tower and Notre Dame Cathedral form Paris' symbolic couple: past and present, stone and metal, sacred and profane. For him, the stone-metal dichotomy is especially important in understanding the new departure the tower stood for. "The history of iron is one of the most progressivist there is; Eiffel crowned that history by making iron the sole material of his constructions and by imagining an object entirely of iron (the tower) raised in the sky of Paris like a stele consecrated to Iron: in this material is synthesized all the Balzacian and Faustian passion of the century." Conceptually, Barthes finds that the tower eludes reason, which demands purpose, by being "fully useless." This frees it from earthbound considerations to play a higher role as a great baroque dream which touches the limits of the irrational . . . In fact, the tower is *nothing*, it achieves a sort of absolute zero as a monument. It is part of no ceremony, not even that of Art. It cannot be visited like a museum, for there is nothing to see *in* the tower. And yet this empty monument receives each year twice as many visitors as the Louvre and many times more than the largest cinema in Paris. Why then does one visit the tower? Doubtless to participate in a dream of which it is more the crystallizer than the object, transforming the touristic rite into an adventure of observation and intelligence . . . Every visitor to the tower becomes a philosophical structuralist without knowing it, spontaneously distinguishing discrete points of Paris and linking and ordering them in his mind: nothing could be less passive than the view of Paris from the tower.

The tower is the ultimate, universal symbol:

> Beyond its role as symbol of Paris, it touches the human imagination in the most general way. Its simple, matrixial form confers on it the vocation of infinite integer: one after the other, depending on our imagination, it becomes the symbol of Paris, of modernity, of communication, of science or the nineteenth century, a rocket, stem, derrick, phallus, lightning rod or insect. In the great domain of dreams, it is the inevitable sign . . . It is impossible to flee this pure sign, *for it means everything.*

The tower's all-embracing symbolism explains the number of suicides on it, he believes, for "despite or because of the innumerable images of life that it gives rise to, it calls down the last image of human experience, that of death."

Barthes is rivaled in the manipulation of heavy theses by Maurice Besset, another French intellectual who has reflected on the Eiffel Tower at length. He sees it as "A monument to itself, created by the century of the mechanistic revolution, the century that overturned all social and aesthetic principles." In particular, Besset describes the tower's builder as "the creator of Eiffelian

223

The tower bristles with antennas of French radio and television networks, the gendarmerie and Paris police.

space," ordering and resolving the rhythms and tensions of forces on the tower with a muscular feeling for space that renders it "an indivisible, living reality, a fluid into which he insinuates himself and against which — the wind — he struggles." Thanks to Eiffel's mastery of "interior and exterior space," the tower becomes for those who behold it "a new form and a new dimension of structured space," inviting the spectator to experience new spatiotemporal relationships. And Besset underlines the coincidence of Eiffel's design of the tower with the era of impressionist painting, both tending toward a dynamic conception of space: the impressionists by breaking down their subjects into pure light, Eiffel by rejecting static masonry for more flexible iron. "It is therefore as a function of an entire aesthetic culture . . . that we see and interpret his tower today."

Inevitably in the land of soaring cathedrals the tower was compared to the work of Gothic builders. "The profound relationship of this art of bolted iron with that of Gothic art" was pointed out by another French writer, who explained:

> The Gothic architects also strived for height. They also supported their vaults with columns, using an absolute minimum of materials. And [like the tower's arches] the walls of their churches are illusory, being no more than filling between the piers. Stand before the great rose windows or the most window-riddled sections of the walls and observe and feel the force lines crossing through the vaults: you will find in these daring leaps a foreshadowing of the aerial art of Eiffel.

But of those who have written about the tower, the man who is perhaps best qualified has expressed his views most simply. Le Corbusier, who found all of Eiffel's designs marked by "an admirable instinct for proportion," had a personal affection for the tower. At the time of the Arts Décoratifs Exposition in Paris in 1925, he wrote that "The Eiffel Tower has entered the domain of architecture. In 1889 it was the aggressive expression of calculations. In 1900 the aesthetes wanted to demolish it. In 1925 it dominates the Arts Déco Exposition. Rising above the plaster palaces with their twisted décor, it looks pure as a crystal." Later, having himself become an architectural legend, Le Corbusier wrote, "I bear witness to the tower as an indefatigable pilgrim who has crisscrossed the world. In the cities, in the savanna, in the pampa, in the desert, on the gats and on the estuaries, everywhere and among the humble as among the others, the tower is in everyone's heart as the sign of a beloved Paris, beloved sign of Paris. Such homage is due to the qualities of a man, of a place and of an epoch."

EPILOGUE

CENOTAPH of the Belle Epoque, cynosure of the postindustrial era, the Eiffel Tower stands today as a watershed emblem. In its time the tower was briefly the man-to-the-moon program of the day, carrying technical innovation to a logical absurdity in order to reassure a nation that had stumbled into defeat. Now it seems rather to represent a culmination of the race's naive enthusiasm for machines in a blissful period ignorant that machines would shortly become machine guns spraying death across the fields of Flanders. The tower's innocent exuberance underscores the brevity of our stay in the Industrial Eden.

Chances are that man's tallest tower will continue to acquire overlays of significance in an age increasingly short of meaning. It may not be far-fetched to relate its role as talisman to a remark Claude Lévi-Strauss, the anthropologist, once made to this writer to the effect that what secular modern man worships more than anything else is his own development and objects that have marked its high points over the ages. Thus the relatively recent veneration of everything antique, from Greek ruins to pre-Columbian art objects to Renaissance paintings, Russian ikons and even old locomotives and automobiles. Similarly, the Eiffel Tower appears to be a growth stock in the nostalgia market.

For the present, it is enough that the tower continue to crane over the Seine, looking old-fashioned and a bit gawky, revealing itself at a glance rather than affronting the world with smug rectangularity. It looks vulnerable in its honesty and one feels affection for it despite its tawdry role as plaything of the masses. The Eiffel Tower reminds us who we were and, by inference, who we are. It is part of us.

ACKNOWLEDGMENTS

MY RESEARCH for this book was greatly facilitated by the generous assistance of M. René Le Grain-Eiffel. Born the year his grandfather's tower was completed, M. Le Grain-Eiffel remains one of the most alert and youthful persons I know. In addition to making available to me in Paris the unpublished memoirs of Gustave Eiffel and a number of other documents difficult of access, he provided many of the illustrations reproduced here. For this I am grateful.

Valued help was also extended by other members of the Eiffel family. Henriette Venot, a granddaughter of Eiffel, and her husband, Louis, kindly opened to me their private collection of Eiffeliana in the village of Salleboeuf, near Bordeaux. Madame André Granet, another granddaughter, lent me certain documents from her personal library in Paris.

The Société de la Tour Eiffel, in the person of its director, M. André Garoux, responded readily to my requests for detailed information. The Bureau International des Expositions in Paris, of which M. René Chalon is secretary general, helpfully put at my disposal its unique library of works on the world's great fairs. Mrs. Mary Meerson of the Cinémathèque at the Musée du Cinema found René Clair's documentary film on the tower for me and arranged a screening. M. Bernard Marrey, head of the new Beaugrenelle municipal library in Paris, assisted me in my search for illustrations.

I wish also to express gratitude to Ellen Joseph, my editor at Houghton Mifflin, who handled the manuscript and illustrations as adroitly as if we had been on the same side of the Atlantic. And special thanks go to my wife, Claudie, for her constant support and for accepting with gracious forbearance my frequent absences from family life in order to write this book.

J.H.

STATISTICS

Number of iron structural components in tower	15,000
Number of rivets	2,500,000
Weight of foundations	277,602 kilograms (306 tons)
Weight of iron	7,341,214 kilograms (8092.2 tons)
Weight of elevator systems	946,000 kilograms (1042.8 tons)
Total weight	8,564,816 kilograms (9441 tons)
Pressure on foundations	4.1 to 4.5 kilograms per square centimeter, depending on pier (58.26 to 64 lbs per square inch)
Height of first platform	57.63 meters (189 feet)
Height of second platform	115.73 meters (379 feet 8 inches)
Height of third platform	276.13 meters (905 feet 11 inches)
Total height in 1889	300.51 meters (985 feet 11 inches)
Total height with television antenna	320.755 meters (1052 feet 4 inches)

Number of steps to top	1671
Maximum sway at top caused by wind	12 centimeters (4¾ inches)
Maximum sway at top caused by metal dilation	18 centimeters (7 inches)
Size of base area	10,281.96 square meters (2.54 acres)
Dates of construction	26 January 1887 to 31 March 1889
Cost of construction	7,799,401.31 francs ($1,505,675.90)
Total number of visitors during Exposition of 1889	1,968,287
Total receipts during Exposition of 1889	5,919,884 francs ($1,142,834.70)

Principal Engineering Projects
of *G. Eiffel et Compagnie*

1865 Train stations at Toulouse and Agen, France

1866 Fine Arts and Archeology pavilions for Paris Exposition of 1867

1867 Bridges for railway line from Poitiers to Limoges, France
to Viaducts at Neuvial and over the Sioule River for Orléans Rail-
1869 way, France
   Church of Notre Dame des Champs, Paris
   Jewish temple, Paris
   Gasworks, Versailles

1870 Bridges for railway lines from Latour to Millau and Brive to
   Tulle, France
   Swing bridge at Dieppe, France

1872 Bridges for railway line from Jassy to Ungheni, Romania
   Harbor installations and customs house for port of Arica, Chile
   Bridges at La Oroya, Peru

1873 Gasworks, La Paz, Bolivia

1874 Locks for dam on Moskva River, Russia

1875 Church at Tacna, Peru
   Church at Manila, Philippines
   Casino at Sables d'Olonne, France

1876 Bridges for Vendée Railway, France
   Bridges for Gerona line, Spain
   Maria Pia Bridge at Oporto, Portugal

1877 Viana Bridge, Portugal
   Train station at Pest, Hungary
   Monumental entrance and City of Paris Pavilion for Paris Ex-
   position of 1878

1878   Bridges for Chemin de Fer du Midi, France
        Bridges for Cáceres line, Spain
        Gasworks at Clichy, France

1879   Bridges for railway from Ploesti to Predeal, Romania
        Bridge at Oued Djemma, Algeria
        Structural work for enlargement of Bon Marché department
        store, Paris
        Annex to Magasins du Louvre department store, Paris

1880   Bridges on Beira Alta line, Portugal
        Bridge over Tagus River, Spain
        Bridges at Binh Dien, Tan An and Ben Luc, Cochin China
        Bridge at Sidi-Moussa, Algeria
        Bridge over Dordogne River at Saint André de Cubzac, France

1881   Bridge over Danube River at Szeged, Hungary
        Headquarters of Crédit Lyonnais bank, Paris
        Train stations at San Sebastián and Santander, Spain
        Dam on Seine River at Port Mort, France
        Interior structure of Statue of Liberty, Paris

1882   Bridge over Dordogne River at Bergerac, France
        Bridges on Asturias line, Spain
        Bridge at Saigon, Cochin China
        Covered market at Bordeaux, France

1883   Bridges over the Tardes River and at Charenton and Sainte
        Claire d'Oloron, France
        Gasworks at Rennes, France

1884   Bridge at Cholon, Cochin China
        Viaduct at Garabit, France
        Steel mill at Pagny-sur-Meuse, France
        Structural work of Galliéra Museum, Paris

1885   Bridges and train stations for line from Lisbon to Cintra,
        Portugal
        Rotating dome for Nice Observatory, France

1889   Thousand-foot tower for Paris Exposition of 1889
        Locks for Panama Canal

NOTES

ONE

page

1 107 governments later. William Shirer, *The Collapse of the Third Republic,* New York, Simon and Schuster, 1969, p. 38.

4 "It divided us least." Shirer, p. 35.

3 Terms of Franco-German settlement and France's payment. Alfred Cobban, Harmondsworth, *A History of Modern France,* Vol. 3, Penguin Books Ltd., 1965, pp. 10–11.

5 As early as 1878. Genesis of the fair is in *L'Exposition de Paris 1889,* Paris, La Librairie Illustrée, 1889.

6 "The participant who can show . . ." Charles Braibant, *Histoire de la Tour Eiffel,* Paris, Librairie Plon, 1964, p. 18.

7 Crystal Palace. James Marston Fitch, *American Building: The Historical Forces that Shaped It,* Vol. 1, Boston, Houghton Mifflin Co., 1966, pp. 140–150.

7 Over six million visitors. This and other attendance figures for world fairs are from Information Document 767 issued by the Bureau International des Expositions, Paris.

8 Prospectus prepared in March 1885. *L'Exposition de Paris 1889,* p. 10.

10 "We will show our sons . . .". *L'Exposition de Paris 1889,* p. 11.

11 Proposals for thousand-foot towers. Eiffel, *La Tour Eiffel en 1900,* Paris, Masson et Cie, 1902, pp. 1–2.

13 Tour Soleil. Charles Cordat, *La Tour Eiffel,* Paris, Les Editions de Minuit, 1955, pp. 19–22.

13 $1.6 million. Eiffel's estimate was eight million francs. Ac-

234

cording to the Banque de France, the exchange rate at that time was 5.18 francs to the dollar; as a general rule I have rounded this to five in calculating dollar figures throughout the book.

14 Teapot tempests. For example the Swiss engineering review "Construire" called Koechlin "the real inventor of the tower" in an article in March 1972.

14 Project first became public in December 1884. Max de Nansouty, "Projet d'une Tour Colossal en Fer de 300 Mètres de Hauteur," Paris, *Le Genie Civil*, December 1884.

16 Eiffel's case against masonry. *La Tour Eiffel en 1900*, p. 3.

16 Advantages of iron. Eiffel, *Les Grandes Constructions Métalliques*, Paris, Imprimerie Chaix, 1888.

17 Eiffel's contract for tower. Alfred Picard, *Exposition Universelle Internationale de 1889 à Paris. Rapport Général*, Paris, Imprimerie Nationale, 1891. Tome Deux, p. 267.

19 "To raise to the glory of modern science . . ." Quoted by Braibant, p. 223.

20–21 Artists' protest. "Les Artistes Contre la Tour Eiffel," *Le Temps*, 14 February 1887.

22 Léon Bloy. Quoted by Jean Keim, *La Tour Eiffel*, Paris, Editions Tel, 1950, p. 7.

23–24 Lockroy's reply to artists. Picard, pp. 270–271.

24 Herbert Hoover shocked an English lady. C. C. Furnas and Joe McCarthy, *The Engineer*, New York, Time, Inc., 1966, p. 33.

25 Eiffel's reply. *Le Temps*, Paris, 14 February 1887.

25 Louis Sullivan himself concluded. Carl W. Condit, *The Rise of the Skyscraper*, Chicago, University of Chicago Press, 1952, p. 44.

TWO

27 Term Industrial Revolution. E. J. Hobsbawm, *The Age of Revolution*, London, Weidenfeld and Nicolson, 1962, p. 28.

28 "Glorious times for the Engineers." Quoted by Hobsbawm, p. 168.

page

28 "If we want any work done . . ." Quoted by Furnas and McCarthy, p. 34.

28 "The 19th century saw three great . . ." Fitch, pp. 140, 167.

29 "The most profound . . ." Carl W. Condit, *American Building,* Chicago, University of Chicago Press, 1968, p. 76.

30 Zola on Les Halles. Quoted by Pierre Schneider, "Paris: Timely Requiem for Les Halles," *The New York Times,* 25 May 1970, p. 42.

30 Mies van der Rohe on Les Halles. Schneider.

30 William Le Baron Jenney et Ecole Centrale. Candit, *Skyscraper,* p. 37.

31–36 Eiffel's ancestry, biography and early career. Eiffel, "Généalogie de la Famille Eiffel; Biographie Industrielle et Scientifique," unpublished, completed in 1923.

33 "They're lots of fun." Quoted by François Poncetton, *Eiffel, le Magicien du Fer,* Paris, Editions de la Tournelle, 1939, p. 60.

THREE

37 "What I need . . ." Poncetton, p. 100.

40 "The architecture of the future." Lewis Mumford, *The Brown Decades,* New York, Harcourt, Brace and Co., 1931, p. 104.

41 Tay Bridge disaster. René Poirier, *The Fifteen Wonders of the World,* New York, Random House, 1961, pp. 228–229.

41–50 Eiffel's bridges and other projects. "Travaux de M. G. Eiffel et Principaux Ouvrages Exécutés par ses Etablissements de 1867 à 1890," appendix to *La Tour Eiffel en 1900,* pp. 323–345.

45 "One of the great victories . . ." Mumford, p. 102.

49 "Liberty Enlightening the World." A good description of the building of the statue is in Oscar Handlin's *Statue of Liberty,* New York, Newsweek Book Division, 1971, pp. 28–48.

52 Valéry's description of great builders. Quoted in Poirier, p. 247.

52–53 "He was pained . . ." Le Corbusier in his preface to Charles Cordat's *La Tour Eiffel.*

236

54–76, All details in my narrative of the tower's construction are from
80–81 Eiffel's definitive account, *La Tour de Trois Cents Mètres*,
Paris, Imprimerie Mercier, 1900.

61 "In almost every case . . ." Robert M. Vogel, "Elevator
Systems of the Eiffel Tower 1889," *United States National
Museum Bulletin*, No. 228, 1961, p. 2.

67 "It is curious and interesting . . ." Quoted by Poncetton, p.
176.

69 To stop construction. Braibant, p. 83.

69 "Modern Tower of Babel." Quoted by Don Cook in "Landmark on the Seine," *Saturday Evening Post*, 11 August 1962,
pp. 26–29.

69 "The Tower Is Sinking." Quoted by Poirier, p. 255.

70 "I was standing at a height . . ." Poirier, p. 252.

70 "New world standards . . ." Fitch, p. 166.

76 "Joined by the belt of girders . . ." *La Tour de Trois Cents
Mètres*, p. 108.

77 International Interoceanic Canal Study Conference. "Bulletin
de la Société de Géographie, juin 1879," Paris Librairie Ch.
Delagrave, 1879. Meeting also described by J. Bouvier, *Les
Deux Scandales de Panama*, Paris, Julliard, 1964, pp. 35–36.

79 Status of Eiffel's work on Panama Canal in 1888. Poncetton,
p. 239.

81 "Judging by the interest . . ." Poncetton, p. 186.

FIVE

82–105 As in the preceding chapter, details of construction are from
La Tour de Trois Cents Mètres.

86–89 "Indian file, with M. Eiffel . . ." *L'Exposition de Paris 1889*,
p. 58.

90–99 A lucid explanation of the tower's elevators and the state of
the art is given by Vogel, "Elevator Systems of the Eiffel
Tower 1889."

94 Charles Otis's telegram to Eiffel. Vogel, p. 28.

95 "Not only safe . . ." Vogel, p. 30.

238

129 "Buffalo Bill, who will be our guest . . ." *Le Figaro*, 16 April 1889.

131 "Each nation, gradually losing its prejudices . . ." *Reports of the U.S. Commissioners*, "General Review of the Sixth Group," p. 8.

134 "I must demand supervision . . ." *Le Figaro*, 15 April 1889.

134 "A painting, before being a warhorse . . ." Quoted in Raymond Rudorff's *Belle Epoque: Paris in the Nineties*, London, Hamish Hamilton, 1972, p. 94.

138 "Here has been shown the glorification . . ." Quoted in *Reports of the U.S. Commissioners*, "Report of the Commissioner-General," p. 19.

138 "This coincidence of the celebration . . ." "Report of the Commissioner-General," p. 20.

138–139 "We have been only too inclined to see . . ." Quoted in *Le Figaro*, 28 October 1889.

139 "Everything connected with the Exposition . . ." *Reports of the U.S. Commissioners*, "Report of the Commissioner-General," p. 27.

140 Quotations from the autographed fan were taken directly from a photograph of it made available to the author by Henriette Venot.

SEVEN

141 "A new idea in Europe." Quoted by Hobsbawm, p. 241.

141 "I hope you may come to know . . ." Palmer White, *Poiret*, London, Studio Vista, 1973, p. 17.

143 "I'd be very stupid . . ." Quoted by Cornelia Otis Skinner, *Elegant Wits and Grand Horizontals*, Boston, Houghton Mifflin Co., 1962, p. 9.

143 "You arrived at your cafe at 1 P.M." Skinner, p. 94.

144 "The harsh smell of gasoline . . ." Skinner, p. 7.

144 "Where luxury is raised to a science." Quoted by Rudorff, p. 33.

145 Number of registered brothels. Rudorff, p. 64.

146 "As an artist . . ." Quoted by Shirer, p. 107.

146 "At one's feet . . ." Quoted by Rudorff, p. 43.

147 Bennett naked on Champs Elysées. Eric Hawkins, *Hawkins of the Paris Herald*, New York, Simon and Schuster, 1963, p. 19.

148 "The permanent glamour of France." Sir Almeric Fitzroy, quoted by Barbara Tuchman, *The Proud Tower*, New York, The Macmillan Company, 1966, p. 171.

149 French birth rate. Ernest Alfred Vizetelly, *Paris and Her People Under the Third Republic*, London, Chatto & Windus, 1919, p. 5.

152 "A mechanism so simple . . ." Poncetton, p. 237.

152 "The day will come . . ." Quoted by Maron J. Simon, *The Panama Affair*, New York, Charles Scribner's Sons, 1971, p. 3.

153 "This man who has lied . . ." Quoted by Simon, p. 102.

154 "There are two categories of Deputies . . ." Simon, p. 107.

155 "The scandal of scandals . . ." Bouvier, p. 7.

156 "You all know who was this obliging . . ." Quoted by Simon, p. 126.

157 Eiffel's statement to judge. Quoted by Poncetton, p. 236.

159 General Février's letter to Eiffel. Reproduced in Eiffel's "Biographie," Tome 1er, p. 37.

160 General Février's letter to the President. Eiffel, "Biographie," pp. 38–40.

160 "An American canal, on American soil." *Encyclopaedia Britannica*, Vol. 17, p. 172C.

EIGHT

161–167 Eiffel's early experiments on the tower are described in his *Travaux Scientifiques Exécutés à la Tour de Trois Cents Mètres*, Paris, Maretheux, 1900.

163 "On rising by elevator . . ." *La Tour de Trois Cents Mètres*, p. 303.

165 "During my engineering career . . ." Eiffel, "Biographie," Tome 3e, p. 1.

166 Santos-Dumont's flight around tower. *La Tour Eiffel en 1900*, pp. 260–266.

167–168 Early aviation experiments and wind tunnels. *The American Heritage History of Flight* (Editor: Alvin M. Josephy, Jr.),

New York, American Heritage Publishing Company, Inc., 1962, pp. 80–81.

172 Bell's speech on presenting Langley Medal. "An Account of the Exercises on the Occasion of the Presentation of the Langley Medal and the Unveiling of the Langley Memorial Tablet, May 6, 1913, including the Addresses." Washington, D.C., The Smithsonian Institution, 1913, pp. 9–10.

172 "Even in thick fog." Ducretet quoted by Poncetton, p. 271.

173–175 Eiffel's honorary decorations. Eiffel, "Biographie," Tome 3ᵉ, pp. 53–54.

174 "Symbol of force and difficulties overcome," Eiffel, "Biographie," Tome 1ᵉʳ, p. 44.

174 "This incomparable monument . . ." Eiffel, "Biographie," Tome 1ᵉʳ, p. 46.

175 Description of Eiffel's town house and life there. Author's interview with René Le Grain-Eiffel.

176 $14 million by 1890. *La Tour de Trois Cents Mètres*, Appendix, p. 4.

176 Eiffel's study reconstructed at Salleboeuf. Author's visit there with Henriette Venot.

177 "I ought to be jealous of the tower . . ." René Le Grain-Eiffel.

177 "Eiffel's voice was soft . . ." Le Corbusier in preface to Cordat.

178 "The illustrious engineer . . ." *Discours Prononcés à L'Inauguration du Monument de Gustave Eiffel, 2 Mai 1929*, Paris, Les Editions Rieder, p. 34.

179 "From my father I inherited . . ." René Le Grain-Eiffel.

NINE

180 "The Crusaders seeing Jerusalem's walls." Quoted by Larry Collins and Dominique Lapierre, *Is Paris Burning?* New York, Simon and Schuster, 1965, p. 236.

181 Sarniguet's race to top. Author's interview with Sarniguet.

182 Germans seized tower June 14, 1940. Information provided by S.T.E.

page

182 Destruction of elevator systems. S.T.E.

184 Ingles's letter to Salles. Shown to author by Madame André Granet.

184 American soldiers on tower. J. Bryan, III, "The Eiffel Tower," *Holiday*, May 1955, pp. 19 et seq.

184 Number of visitors to tower, 1889 to present. Figures provided by S.T.E.

185 Tower admissions compared to other French monuments. Figures provided by French National Tourist Office, Paris.

186 Income figures for tower. S.T.E.

186 Painting the tower. Information provided by contractor, La Seigneurie, in Paris suburb of Bobigny.

187 Debate over tower's color. *Le Figaro*, 3 May 1968.

187 "Must Tower be Razed?"; "Tower in Good Health." *Le Monde*, 10–11 October 1972.

190 Biggest illuminated advertising sign ever. *Guinness Book of World Records*, p. 308.

190 Jacopozzi's lights. Documents provided by Citroën public relations office, Paris.

192 Lindbergh sights the tower. Charles A. Lindbergh, *The Spirit of St. Louis*, New York, Charles Scribner's Sons, 1953, p. 487.

195 Peugeot wanted space. *Le Figaro*, 8 July 1968.

196 Comte de Lambert's flight. *L'Illustration*, 23 October 1909.

196 Up the tower on stilts. Braibant, p. 180.

196 Footrace. Braibant; also Don Cook.

196 Bicycle on stairs. Jacques Morlaine, *La Tour Eiffel Inconnue*, Paris, Librairie Hachette, 1971, p. 112.

196 Up on one leg. *Le Figaro*, 4 June 1959.

197 Collot crashes. Morlaine, p. 115.

197 German student climbs. *Le Figaro*, 9 July 1954.

197 Mountain climbers on seventy-fifth anniversary. Genêt, "Letter from Paris," *The New Yorker*, 16 May 1964; also "Now Man Conquers Mt. Eiffel," *Life*, 5 June 1964.

198 Artificial ski slope. *L'Aurore*, 12 September 1969.

198 Streaking at the tower. *Le Monde*, 9 March 1974.

198 First suicide. Braibant, p. 181.

199 Suicides on Golden Gate Bridge. "The Bridge of Sighs," *Newsweek*, 13 August 1973.

199 Teichelt's suicide. Morlaine, pp. 107–110.

242

page

199 Woman leaps from third platform. Braibant, p. 181.

200 Incorrigible suicide. Morlaine, pp. 131–133.

200 Change of mind. Morlaine, pp. 131–133.

201 Woman gives birth. Braibant, p. 181.

201 Woman lands on car. Morlaine, p. 129.

201 "All three would be ugly . . ." *Le Figaro*, 14 October 1964.

202 April Fool's jokes. Morlaine, p. 122; *Paris-Presse-L'In-transigeant*, 1 April 1964.

202 Fire on tower. *Le Figaro*, 4 January 1956.

203 "Paris will forever miss . . ." *Le Figaro*, 20 June 1957.

203 Prussian con man 1891. Braibant, p. 180.

203 Lustig "sells" tower. James F. Johnson and Floyd Miller, *The Man Who Sold the Eiffel Tower*, New York, Doubleday & Co., 1961.

204 "U.S. Go Home." *Le Figaro*, 8 April 1967.

204 TV set thrown off. *Le Figaro*, 1 February 1968.

204 NLF dynamite attempt. *Le Figaro*, 24 September 1958.

205 SAO bomb plans. Braibant, p. 182.

205 1939 beauty contest. Morlaine, p. 99.

205 Automobile to twenty-five millionth visitor. Henry Giniger, "Monsieur Eiffel's Fancy," *The New York Times Magazine*, 7 June 1953.

205 Automobile to thirty-five millionth visitor. *Le Figaro*, 1 July 1959.

205 Seventy-fifth anniversary. "Cashing in on its 75 Years," *Business Week*, 16 May 1964.

206 Letters to the tower. Shown to the author by S.T.E. officials.

TEN

207 Antenna near Fargo, N.D. Information provided by station KTHI-TV.

207 Moscow and Toronto towers. *Guinness Book of World Records*, p. 290.

209 Baker's project for Wembley. Braibant, p. 167.

209 Chicago tower project. *La Petite Architecture*, 1 November 1932.

page

209 St. Louis Gateway Arch. *Guinness Book of World Records*, p. 302.

209 Nicolas Schoffer's scheme. *International Herald Tribune*, 6 June 1972.

211 Replica in King's Mill, Ohio. Information provided by S.T.E.

211 Miami's project. S.T.E.

211 Montreal projects for Expo 67. Public Relations Department, City of Montreal; *Le Figaro*, 6 July 1965.

211 Importing the Eiffel Tower to Myrtle Beach. *Atlanta Constitution*, 22 January 1974.

212 Lawsuit over tower souvenirs. Morlaine, pp. 115–120; Poncetton, p. 221.

212 Surveys of Paris department stores. *Le Figaro*, 22 July 1964.

212 Model Eiffel Tower in Buenos Aires. *Le Figaro*, 6 September 1963.

212 Watchmaker's model. *Le Figaro*, 21 September 1971.

213 Model of perforated aluminum. Information provided by S.T.E.

213 Howard Porter's model. Author's interview with Mr. Porter.

213 Roger Blough's remarks. Transcript provided by Public Relations Department, United States Steel.

214 Text on plaque. United States Steel.

214 John Hancock Skystone. Information provided by Public Information Department, John Hancock Mutual Life Insurance Company.

214 "All in all, this audacious construction . . ." *L'Echo de Paris*, 4 January 1924.

215 Crédit Lyonnais advertisement. *Fortune*, October 1971.

215 "The surprising thing . . ." Roland Barthes, *La Tour Eiffel*, Paris, Delpire Editeur, 1964, p. 73.

215 "Notre Dame represents the Faith . . ." *Le Figaro*, 30 December 1971.

216 Early songs about the tower. Braibant, p. 200.

216 "We know that by night . . ." Poem by André Muller in *Le Gaulois*, 16 June 1917.

216 Mistinguette's review. Morlaine, p. 144.

217 "Notre Dame of the Left Bank . . . the queen of Paris." Quoted by Morlaine, p. 139.

217 "A cage of bluebirds": Morlaine, p. 138.

244

217 "Shepherdess, O Eiffel Tower." Quoted by Kiem, p. 7.

217 "Hello world . . ." Quoted by Braibant, p. 191.

217 "The staircase to infinity." Quoted by Morlaine, p. 138.

217 "The *i* of Paris . . ." Quoted by Poirier, p. 238.

217 "I can hear the Eiffel Tower . . ." Poirier, p. 238.

217 "The thousand acres . . ." Quoted by Braibant, p. 189.

218 "Purely dynamic conception . . ." Maurice Besset, *Gustave Eiffel*, Paris, Librairie A. Hatier, 1957, unpaged.

220 "In 1911 Delaunay did . . ." Quoted by Morlaine, p. 137.

220 "From the only place . . ." *Le Figaro*, 6 May 1955.

222 René Clair. Quoted in *Le Figaro*, 20 June 1974.

222 "European civilization . . ." Speech to conference, "Les Valeurs Européennes," Strasbourg, July 1962.

222 "The history of iron . . ." Barthes, p. 60.

222 "Fully useless." Barthes, p. 27.

223 "A great baroque dream . . ." Barthes, p. 28.

223 "The tower is *nothing* . . ." Barthes, p. 33.

223 "Every visitor . . ." Barthes, p. 43.

223 "Beyond its role as symbol . . ." Barthes, p. 27.

223 "The last image of human experience . . ." Barthes, p. 82.

223 "A monument to itself . . ." Besset.

223 "The creator of Eiffelian space." Besset.

225 "An indivisible . . ." Besset.

225 "Interior and exterior space." Besset.

225 "A new form . . ." Besset.

225 "It is therefore . . ." Besset.

225 "The profound relationship . . ." Poncetton, p. 219.

225 "An admirable instinct . . ." Le Corbusier in his preface to Cordat.

225 "The Eiffel Tower has entered the domain . . ." Le Corbusier, *L'Art Décoratif d'Aujourd'hui*, Paris, Les Editions G. Crès et Cie., 1925, p. 141.

226 "I bear witness to the tower . . ." Le Corbusier in his preface to Cordat.

BIBLIOGRAPHY

"An Account of the Exercises on the Occasion of the Presentation of the Langley Medal and the Unveiling of the Langley Memorial Tablet, May 6, 1913, including the Addresses." Washington: The Smithsonian Institution, 1913.

"Les Artistes Contre la Tour Eiffel." "Résumé de Conversation avec Monsieur Eiffel." *Le Temps,* 14 February 1887.

Barral, Georges and Jacques. *Histoire Populaire des 72 Savants de la Tour Eiffel.* Paris: J. Mersch, 1889.

· Barthes, Roland. *La Tour Eiffel.* Paris: Delpire Editeur, 1964.

· Barry, Joseph. "Eiffel, Versatile Engineer-Builder of Towering Talents." *Smithsonian,* April 1972, pp. 49–53.

Besset, Maurice. *Eiffel.* Paris: Hatier, 1957.

Billings, Henry. *Bridges.* New York: The Viking Press, 1956.

Blough, Roger M. Remarks on occasion of dedication of Unisphere and first ground-breaking at New York World's Fair site, 6 March 1963.

Blume, Mary. "The Showman from Paris." *International Herald Tribune,* 22 December 1973.

Bouvier, J. *Les Deux Scandales de Panama.* Paris: Julliard, 1964.

Braibant, Charles. *Histoire de la Tour Eiffel.* Paris: Librairie Plon, 1964.

· Bryan, J. "The Eiffel Tower." *Holiday,* May 1955, pp. 19 et seq.

"Bulletin de la Société de Géographie, juin 1879." Paris: Librairie Ch. Delagrave, 1879.

"Cashing In on Its 75 years." *Business Week,* 16 May 1964, p. 31.

Cobban, Alfred. *A History of Modern France.* 3 vols. Harmondsworth: Penguin Books Ltd., 1965.

Collins, Larry, and Lapierre, Dominique. *Is Paris Burning?* New York: Simon and Schuster, 1965.

246

Condit, Carl W. *American Building*. Chicago: University of Chicago Press, 1968.

————. *The Rise of the Skyscraper*. Chicago: University of Chicago Press, 1952.

Cook, Don. "Landmark on the Seine." *Saturday Evening Post*, 11 August 1962, pp. 26–29.

Cordat, Charles. *La Tour Eiffel*. Paris: Les Editions de Minuit, 1955.

Dansette, A. *Les Affaires de Panama*. Paris: Perrin, 1934.

d'Aragon, Marie. *Paris, Tour Eiffel*. Paris: Grange Batelière, 1973.

de Nansouty, Max. *Projet d'une Tour Colossal en Fer de 300 Mètres de Hauteur*. Paris: Le Génie Civil, 1884.

De Vries, Leonard. *Victorian Inventions*. New York: American Heritage Press, 1971.

Eiffel, Gustave. *Notice sur le Pont du Douro à Porto*. Paris: Paul Dupont, 1879.

————. *Notice sur les différents types des ponts portatifs, system Eiffel*. Paris, 1885.

————. *Notice sur le Viaduc de Garabit (près Saint Flour)*. Paris: Paul Dupont, 1888.

————. *Les Grandes Constructions Métalliques*. Paris: Imprimerie Chaix, 1888.

————. "Conference sur la Tour de trois cents mètres faite à la Société Centrale du Travail Professionel à l'Ecole des Hautes Etudes Commerciales, 20 novembre 1889." Paris, 1889.

————. *La Tour de Trois Cents Mètres*. Paris: Imprimerie Mercier, 1900.

————. *Travaux Scientifiques Exécutés à la Tour de Trois Cents Mètres*. Paris: Maretheux, 1900.

————. *La Tour Eiffel en 1900*. Paris: Masson et Cie, 1902.

————. *Dix Années d'Observations Météorologiques à Sèvres (S. & O.) de 1892 à 1901*. Paris: Maretheux, 1904.

————. *Recherches Experimentales sur la Résistance de l'Air Exécutées à la Tour Eiffel*. Paris: Maretheux, 1907.

————. *Inauguration du Nouveau Laboratoire Aérodynamique*. Paris: Maretheux, 1912.

————. *The Resistance of the Air and Aviation*. Boston: Houghton Mifflin Co., 1913.

————. *Etudes sur l'Hélice Aérienne, faites au Laboratoire d'Auteuil*. Paris: E. Chiron, Librairie Aéronautique, 1920.

————. "Généalogie de la Famille Eiffel; Biographie Industrielle et Scientifique," 4 vols., unpublished, completed in 1923.

"Eiffel Tower for Myrtle Beach?" *Atlanta Constitution*, 22 January 1974.

The Eiffel Tower Report of the Smithsonian Institution. Washington, D.C., 1889.

L'Exposition de Paris 1889. Paris: La Librairie Illustrée, 1889.

Exposition Universelle Internationale de 1889 à Paris. Catalogue Général Officiel. Lille: Imprimerie L. Danel, 1889.

Ferrié, Guillet, Lemarchand and Martin. *Discours Prononcés à l'Inauguration du Monument de G. Eiffel, 2 mai 1929*. Paris, 1929.

Fitch, James Marston. *American Building: The Historical Forces That Shaped It*. Vol. 1. Boston: Houghton Mifflin Co., 1966.

Furnas, C. C. and McCarthy, Joe. *The Engineer*. New York: Time, Inc., 1966.

Genêt. "Letter from Paris: Seventy-fifth Anniversary of Eiffel Tower." *The New Yorker*, 16 May 1964, pp. 176–177.

Giniger, Henry. "Monsieur Eiffel's Fancy." *The New York Times Magazine*, 7 June 1953.

"Gold Mine in the Sky." *Newsweek*, 18 June 1962, pp. 69–70.

"I Grandi Viodotti di Eiffel nel Massif Central." *Zodiac 13: International Magazine of Contemporary Architecture*. Milan: Edizioni di Comunità, n.d.

Guy, Christian. *Une Tour Nommée Eiffel*. Paris: Presses de la Cité, 1957.

Handlin, Oscar. *Statue of Liberty*. New York: Newsweek Book Division, 1971.

Hawkins, Eric. *Hawkins of the Paris Herald*. New York: Simon and Schuster, 1963.

Henderson, W. O. *The Industrialization of Europe 1780–1914*. London: Thames & Hudson, 1969.

Hobsbawm, E. J. *The Age of Revolution*. London: Weidenfeld and Nicolson, 1962.

Igot, Yves. *Gustave Eiffel*. Paris: Didier, 1962.

Inauguration du Nouveau Laboratoire Aéro-dynamique de M. G. Eiffel, 19 mars 1912. Paris: Maretheux, 1912.

Johnson, James F. and Miller, Floyd. *The Man Who Sold the Eiffel Tower*. New York: Doubleday and Co., 1961.

Josephy, Alvin M., Jr., ed. *The American Heritage History of Flight*. New York: American Heritage Publishing Co., 1962.

"Jumping-Off Place." *Time*, 9 September 1966, p. 37.

Keim, Jean. *La Tour Eiffel.* Paris: Editions Tel, 1950.

Le Corbusier. *L'Art Décoratif d'Aujourd'hui.* Paris: Les Editions G. Crès et Cie., 1925.

Le Grain-Eiffel, René. Speech at centennial of first Eiffel viaducts. Château de Rochefort, Gannat, 16 August 1969.

———. "Gustave Eiffel et son Oeuvre." Speech at opening of Lycée Technique Gustave Eiffel in Bordeaux, 26 November 1970.

Lindbergh, Charles A. *The Spirit of St. Louis.* New York: Charles Scribner's Sons, 1953.

Mandell, Richard D. *Paris 1900: the Great World's Fair.* Toronto: University of Toronto Press, 1967.

Maupassant, Guy de. *La Vie Errante.* Paris: Ernest Flammarion, Editeur, 1925.

McCullough, David. *The Great Bridge.* New York: Simon and Schuster, 1972.

McWhirter, Norris and Ross. *The Guinness Book of Records.* 12th U.S. ed., New York: Sterling Publishing Co., 1973.

Mock, Elizabeth B. *The Architecture of Bridges.* New York: The Museum of Modern Art, 1949.

Morlaine, Jacques. *La Tour Eiffel Inconnue.* Paris: Librairie Hachette, 1971.

Mumford, Lewis. *Sticks and Stones.* New York: W. W. Norton & Co., 1924.

———. *The Brown Decades.* New York: Harcourt, Brace and Co., 1931.

"Now Man Conquers Mt. Eiffel." *Life,* 5 June 1964, pp. 108–10.

"L'Ouverture de L'Exposition." *Le Figaro,* 7 May 1889.

"Paris Recalls Building of 'Loathsome' Eiffel Tower." *Life,* 3 July 1950, pp. 2–4.

Peissi, P. *Eiffel.* Paris: Editions du Verger, 1946.

Picard, Alfred. *Exposition Universelle Internationale de 1889 à Paris. Rapport Général.* Paris: Imprimerie Nationale, 1891.

Poirier, René. *The Fifteen Wonders of the World.* New York: Random House, 1961.

Poncetton, François. *Eiffel, le Magicien du Fer.* Paris: Editions de la Tournelle, 1939.

Prévost, Jean. *Eiffel.* Paris: Les Editions Rieder, 1929.

Reports of the United States Commissioners to the Universal Exposition of 1889. Washington: Government Printing Office, 1890.

Rousselet, Louis. *L'Exposition Universelle de 1889*. Paris: Librairie Hachette et Cie., 1890.

Rudorff, Raymond. *Belle Epoque: Paris in the Nineties*. London: Hamish Hamilton, 1972.

Schneider, Pierre. "Paris: Timely Requiem for Les Halles." *New York Times*, 25 May 1970, p. 42.

Shirer, William. *The Collapse of the Third Republic*. New York: Simon and Schuster, 1969.

Simon, Maron J. *The Panama Affair*. New York: Charles Scribner's Sons, 1971.

Skinner, Cornelia Otis. *Elegant Wits and Grand Horizontals*. Boston: Houghton Mifflin Co., 1962.

Sondern, Frederic, Jr. "Monsieur Eiffel and His Wonderful Tower." *The Reader's Digest*, June 1954, pp. 103–107.

Tuchman, Barbara W. *The Proud Tower*. New York: The Macmillan Co., 1966.

Vizetelly, Ernest Alfred. *Paris and Her People under the Third Republic*. London: Chatto & Windus, 1919.

Vogel, Robert M. "Elevator Systems of the Eiffel Tower 1889." *United States National Museum Bulletin*, no. 228, 1961.

Weil, B. *Panama*. Paris: Grasset, 1934.

White, Palmer. *Poiret*. London: Studio Vista, 1973.

INDEX

construction of Sioule bridge by, 41–42; construction of bridge over Douro at Oporto by, 41–44; construction of bridge over Truyère at Garabit by, 44–46; other constructions undertaken by, 47–49; contribution of, to design of Statue of Liberty, 49–52; and construction of Panama Canal, 76–80; on usefulness of Eiffel Tower, 100–102; and completion of tower, 105–7; and opening of 1889 Exposition, 110; and impact of tower, 139–40; and Panama scandal, 152–54, 157–60, 161; weather experiments conducted by, 161–66; involvement of, in aviation, 166–72; interest of, in communications, 172–73; later years of, 173–77; death of, 177, 214; memorial for and recognition of, 177–79; and fire in tower, 202; and lawsuit over tower souvenirs, 212; Le Corbusier on tower and, 225–26. *See also* Eiffel Tower

255

199, 200–201, 202; presentations by, to milestone visitors to tower, 205; letters received by, 206
Souvenirs and replicas, of Eiffel Tower, 212–13
Statue of Liberty, 185; Eiffel's contributions to design of, 49–52, 119
S.T.E., see Société de la Tour Eiffel
Suez Canal, Eiffel's visit to, 37–38
Suicides, on Eiffel Tower, 198–202, 223
Sullivan, Louis, 25, 30

Talleyrand, 54–55
Tay Bridge disaster (Scotland), 41
Teichelt (French tailor), 199
Thiers, Adolphe, 3, 4
Third Republic, 2, 149
Tillo, Alfredo M., 129
Tirard, Pierre, 105, 107, 138; and opening of 1889 Exposition, 108, 111
Toronto tower, 207
Toulouse-Lautrec, 145
Tour Maine-Montparnasse, 208
Trevithick, Richard, 10, 24
Triffoz, Armand, 204–5
Tuchman, Barbara, 148

Unisphere, 213–14
United States, participation of, in 1889 Paris Exposition, 126–29
United States Steel Corporation, 213
Utrillo, Maurice, 218, 220

Valéry, Paul, 52
Van Dongen, Kess, 218
Vauban, Sébastien Le Prestre de, 178
Venot, Henriette, 176
Verlaine, Paul, 146
Victoria, Queen, 110, 118
Vitel, Georges, 212–13
Vladimir (Grand Duke of Russia), 118
Vogel, Robert M., 61
Voltaire, 177

Waldeck-Rousseau, Pierre, 157
Washington Monument, 10, 16, 17, 105, 185
Watt, James, 24
Weather, experiments conducted by Eiffel on, 161–66
Weil, Count, 118
Wenham, F. H., 168
William IV (King of England), 10
Wimpffen, Count, 151
Windsor, Duke and Duchess of, 205
World's fair, 6–8
Wren, Christopher, 177
Wright, Wilbur and Orville, 171

Young, Thomas, 40

Zettelmaier (worker on Eiffel Tower), 85
Zola, Emile, 30, 146, 150–51, 177

257